WHO *IS* JESUS?

ALSO BY J. V. FESKO

WHO *IS* JESUS?

Knowing Christ through His "I Am" Sayings

J. V. Fesko

Reformation Heritage Books
Grand Rapids, MI

Who Is Jesus?
© 2016 J. V. Fesko

Reformation Heritage Books
2965 Leonard St. NE
Grand Rapids, MI 49525
616-977-0889 / Fax 616-285-3246
e-mail: orders@heritagebooks.org
website: www.heritagebooks.org

Printed in the United States of America
16 17 18 19 20 21/10 9 8 7 6 5 4 3 2 1

Library of Congress Cataloging-in-Publication Data

Names: Fesko, J. V., 1970- author.
Title: Who is Jesus? : knowing Christ through his "I am" sayings / J.V. Fesko.
Description: Grand Rapids, Michigan : Reformation Heritage Books, 2016.
Identifiers: LCCN 2016027146 (print) | LCCN 2016028130 (ebook) | ISBN 9781601784872 (pbk. : alk. paper) | ISBN 9781601784889 (epub)
Subjects: LCSH: Jesus Christ—Person and offices—Biblical teaching. | Bible. John--Criticism, interpretation, etc. | Jesus Christ—Words. | Jesus Christ.
Classification: LCC BT203 .F47 2016 (print) | LCC BT203 (ebook) | DDC 232—dc23
LC record available at https://lccn.loc.gov/2016027146

For additional Reformed literature, request a free book list from Reformation Heritage Books at the above regular or e-mail address.

To
Wally and Beth King

Contents

Preface

Most preachers have favorite books of the Bible, and that includes me. For many reasons, the gospel of John is one of my favorites: it is rich in imagery, thick with theological significance, and bursting at the seams with a message that requires great meditation. I'm not implying that other books of the Bible do not bear the same characteristics; I simply have a particular interest in John's gospel.

I first seriously studied the book of John when I was in Scotland doing my postgraduate work. I wanted to study the Bible even though I was immersed in researching sixteenth- and seventeenth-century Reformed theology for my doctoral dissertation. John's gospel made a tremendous impact on me then as it does now.

I again took up my study of John during my pastorate, when I preached through the book beginning in the spring of 2008. One thing I tried to impress on my congregation was John's numerous and rich allusions and connections to the Old Testament. Far too many of us read the New Testament unaware of how often the authors employ the Old Testament. At the time I likened John's frequent allusions to the Old Testament to Joseph's coat of many colors. I told my church that Jesus regularly donned this beautiful coat of Old Testament themes, images, and passages to show the people around Him His true identity—that He was and is the Son of God—God in the flesh—and the long-awaited fulfillment of Old Testament promises and prophecies.

I borrow, if you will, the idea of Joseph's coat of many colors, though I am not arguing that there is an interpretive or exegetical connection between Joseph's coat and Jesus's continual references to the Old Testament. Rather, I simply borrow the idea because Joseph's coat was a sign of his father's favor—it was costly and beautiful. In a similar fashion, the Father ordained all of redemptive history to point to His Son; He prepared a rich and costly robe for His Son, and the Son put it on when He became incarnate and walked the dusty roads of Israel. He may have looked like an ordinary man, as many assumed that He was, but with the Spirit-wrought eyes of faith, God's people could see this magnificent coat.

I hope and pray, therefore, that this little book will be a source of encouragement to the broader church. Too many believers are plagued by doubts about who Jesus is. Is He truly God in the flesh? John gives a resounding yes to this question! I also believe this book can serve as a useful tool for evangelism. Do you know anyone who wants to know who Jesus claimed to be? Is He merely a moral teacher, or is He God in the flesh? John's gospel gives us a clear answer to this question, and I hope I have captured at least a glimmer of the glorious truth he sets forth.

I want to note that two sources were of immense help in the preparation of this book: D. A. Carson's commentary on John's gospel, and the *New Testament Commentary on the Use of the Old Testament*, edited by G. K. Beale and

D. A. Carson. Serious students of the Bible would benefit greatly from owning a copy of this wonderful commentary.

Thank you, Jay Collier, for inviting me to write this book, and Dr. Beeke, for your willingness to publish it. Thanks to both of you for your continued interest in and encouragement of my work. I owe thanks to Annette Gysen for her keen editorial eye and her helpful suggestions for ways to improve my unpolished manuscript. I am grateful to my family: to my wife, Anneke, and my three bairns—Val and Rob, my lads, and Carmen, my wee lass and all-around crazy woman. Thank you, dear family, for your love and encouragement and for your willingness to forgive me when I sin against you. I hope and pray, dear family, that you will meditate on the themes in this little book and that you will write them on the walls of your hearts.

I dedicate this book to Wally and Beth King—good friends, fellow servants in Christ's church, and all-around fun people. From the first moment that you met me, you showed me love, warm hospitality, and friendship. From the first moment you met Anneke, you warmly received her and treated her like a long-lost friend. You have shown great love for my children, continually bathing them in care and attention. You have also continued faithfully to serve Christ's church—Wally, in your service as an elder for nearly three decades, and Beth, in your continual sacrificial service to the church in whatever area you can. Our family is grateful for your friendship, and it is to both of you that I dedicate this book.

Introduction: Son of God, or Merely Man?

Who is Jesus? Is He the Son of God? Is He God incarnate? Is He merely a man that the church has mistakenly identified as God? These are some of the questions that naturally surround Jesus's identity. The church has claimed for nearly two millennia that Jesus is God in the flesh. Every Lord's Day, many Christians today profess the Nicene Creed, which was written in AD 325. As we recite this ancient creed, we join hands with our ancestors and collectively profess the deity of Christ, that He is "the only-begotten Son of God, begotten of his Father before all worlds, God of God, Light of Light, very God of very God, begotten, not made, being of one substance with the Father; by whom all things were made." Such claims are catholic; that is, they are universal—Christians everywhere profess the deity of Christ. In spite of this universally confessed truth, there are often two types of responses.

The first type of response comes from unbelievers who deny key tenets of the faith such as Christ's divinity. The second type of response comes from the Christian believer who willingly affirms the deity of Christ but might be hard pressed to demonstrate it from Scripture. Such a person might rightly point to the opening verse of

John's gospel to prove the deity of Christ: "In the beginning was the Word, and the Word was with God, and the Word was God" (1:1). But if he is asked to show other passages that demonstrate Christ's deity, he is stumped. He might rightly appeal to Jesus's miracles, such as when He walked on water or raised Lazarus from the dead. But often Christians appeal to these kinds of passages merely because they know that only God can do things such as walk on water or raise the dead—certainly no human being is capable of such feats.

Christians are correct in these conclusions, but what many do not realize is that there is much more to these passages of Scripture. Imagine rummaging through your attic and discovering an old gold coin. You mount the coin in a frame and hang it on your wall because you want an antique decoration for your office. You know it is a valuable coin because it is made of gold, it is old, and it is in good condition. You suspect that it might be worth a lot of money, but you do not investigate the matter further because you are content with your new office decoration. A few months later a friend walks into your office and notices the coin hanging on your wall and gasps. "Where did you get this coin? This is a 1931 Saint-Gaudens double eagle twenty-dollar gold coin! This could easily be worth over one hundred thousand dollars!" You knew the coin was valuable, perhaps worth a few thousand dollars, but you did not know it was *this* valuable. Such is the nature of our appeal to the miracles of Christ. They are certainly valuable and important pieces of evidence that establish Christ's identity, but most people do not realize how valuable they are.

Many Christians examine Christ's statements and actions and do not realize that they actually gaze on things that have roots that stretch back to the Old Testament and, as such, have great significance. What would people think if a politician today donned a top hat, a black suit, and sported a chin curtain beard, walked out onto the floor of the Senate, and said, "Four score and seven years ago our fathers brought forth on this continent, a new nation"? Without knowing the actual identity of the politician, people would recognize that he was invoking Abraham Lincoln, the sixteenth president of the United States. Many Americans are familiar with Lincoln's famous Gettysburg Address, and they know of Lincoln's dress and grooming habits from pictures they have seen in various history books. Informed American citizens would immediately understand the politician's actions and would know that he was trying to connect his actions with the nation's history and cloak his policies with the historical legitimacy of a well-respected president.

While Jesus was not a politician, He conducted his ministry in Israel cloaked in what I call His coat of many Old Testament colors. He did not arrive on the earth devoid of a personal history. Rather, for ages God's people had eagerly looked forward to the day when the promised seed of the woman would crush the head of the serpent (Gen. 3:15). Old Testament prophets foretold of the Messiah; God foreordained events, people, and places to foreshadow the person and work of His Son. God the Father created a beautiful coat stitched together by the threads of His holy providence and made of different prophecies, promises, images, themes, and ideas

that would become manifest in His Son upon His arrival.
Jesus walked onto the stage of history, donned this coat,
and performed the script that His Father gave Him.

People who read the Bible with attention to Christ's
Old Testament coat can see many familiar passages of
Scripture with fresh eyes. They no longer behold merely
an old gold coin but perceive an amazingly rare and highly
valuable antique. They no longer view Christ's miracles as
bare manifestations of divine power but as the fulfillment
of Old Testament promises. Suddenly they recognize
that the New Testament shouts from the rooftops, "Jesus
the Messiah is here! God in the flesh has come to dwell
among men! You can see and know this because He
wears the coat of His Father—His coat of many Old
Testament colors!"

One way to see the vividness of Christ's coat is to
examine the "I am" sayings of Jesus in the gospel of John.
There are fourteen places in John's gospel where Jesus says
the words "I am," which sometimes stand alone as a title
when He invokes the divine name for Himself. In other
words, when Jesus says, "Before Abraham was, I AM"
(John 8:58), He is taking for Himself the sacred name of
Yahweh revealed to Moses at the burning bush (Ex. 3:14)
and is claiming to be God. Other times Jesus invokes
the words "I am" and then follows them with a com-
plement—a word or phrase that completes His thought.
He says He is the bread of life (6:35, 48); the light of the
world (8:12); the door (10:9); the good shepherd (10:11);
the resurrection and the life (11:25); the way, the truth,
and the life (14:6); and the true vine (15:1). Each of these
statements reveals something about who Jesus is, but they

chiefly reveal that Jesus is the great I AM. God in the
flesh has come down to dwell among men and to seek and
save the lost.

We should also note that John intertwines Jesus's "I
am" sayings with the seven signs of His divinity that he
presents in his gospel:

- Turning water into wine (2:1–11)
- Healing a nobleman's son (4:46–54)
- Healing a lame man (5:1–15)
- Feeding the crowd of five thousand (6:1–14)
- Walking on water (6:16–21)
- Healing the man born blind (9:1–7)
- Raising Lazarus from the dead (11:1–45)

Each of these miracles served as a signpost that identified Jesus as the long-awaited Messiah—the fulfillment
of God's covenant promises. Combined, the seven signs
and the "I am" sayings present a rich account of Christ's
claims that He was indeed God in the flesh. While the
seven signs are definitely worthy of investigation in their
own right, my focus in this book is Jesus's "I am" sayings.[1]

In each successive chapter we will examine the fourteen different "I am" sayings of Jesus so that we can
have a better understanding of who Jesus is and who
He claimed to be. We will keep a close eye on Christ's
Old Testament coat of many colors so that we can have a

---

1. See Anthony T. Selvaggio, *The Seven Signs: Seeing the Glory of
Christ in the Gospel of John* (Grand Rapids: Reformation Heritage Books,
2010).

better and deeper understanding of His claims. In the light of the Old Testament, we will see Jesus in His biblical glory and recognize that we must fall down and worship Him as God in the flesh.

CHAPTER 1

The Great I AM
John 6:16–21

[Jesus] said to them, "It is I; do not be afraid."
—JOHN 6:20

This world's seas are among nature's most beautiful features—they are filled with rich blue hues and amazing creatures both great and small. Also, they provide the setting for one of creation's greatest portraits—the burst of the sun as it rises in the east and its slow descent of beauty as it hides beneath the western seas. Even though the sea provides scenes of splendor, it can also be one of nature's most terrifying places. As quickly as the sea lulls you into a sense of peace, it can fill your heart with terror with its rising swells and its churning waters that can consume vessels large and small.

The disciples found themselves in this scenario: they set out on a calm Sea of Galilee to head across to Capernaum, but a great wind began blowing. What they undoubtedly thought would be an uneventful nighttime journey turned into a potentially disastrous nightmare. They thought their lives would probably be lost until they encountered Jesus on the storm-tossed sea. They saw Jesus walking on water!

Many people look at this miracle as simply a suspension of the laws of physics, and then they move on. However, this miracle goes far beyond the suspension of the laws of physics, as Jesus dons His coat of many Old Testament images, themes, and colors to inform His disciples of His divine identity. He stood on the water and told His disciples, "Fear not, I AM." In this first of Jesus's "I am" sayings, He shows us through John's gospel how the entire Old Testament was written about Him. But more specifically, in the midst of this miracle, Jesus identifies Himself as the great I AM. Only when we recognize Christ's identity as the great I AM can we know that our Lord and Savior cares and provides for our every need. He will always be faithful to get us to our final destination—the goal of our earthly pilgrimage.

Jesus Walks on Water

The passage begins somewhat mundanely as darkness falls on the disciples and they get into a boat to return to the other side of the Sea of Galilee (6:16–17). John gives us a clue of what is to come: the presence of darkness and the absence of Jesus signal that, like eerie background music, danger is ahead. John thematically links the ideas of light and dark throughout his gospel; Nicodemus came to Jesus, the light of the world, at night (3:2); and Jesus was betrayed at night (13:30). It is dark, and Jesus is not there. John is letting us know that something will happen soon.

It is a familiar story: The Sea of Galilee becomes storm-tossed, and the disciples fear for their lives. Being on the water on a dark night can send fear into the hearts of the most fearless of men. Moreover, we see in verse 19 that the disciples had rowed about three or four miles out into the sea, which means that in such stormy waters, they were well beyond the shore and incapable of swimming to safety should the boat sink. In the middle of this stormy night, as the waves lash the disciples' tiny boat, they see in the darkness what they at first think is a ghost (see Matt. 14:26; Mark 6:49). It is not a ghost, but Jesus walking on the water to join them. As He joins the disciples, He wears His Old Testament coat of many colors.

Job describes Yahweh:

> He removes the mountains, and they do not know
> When He overturns them in His anger;
> He shakes the earth out of its place,
> And its pillars tremble;
> He commands the sun, and it does not rise;
> He seals off the stars;
> He alone spreads out the heavens,
> *And treads on the waves of the sea.*
>   (Job 9:5–8, emphasis added)

When John describes Jesus walking on the water in verse 19, his vocabulary is similar to the Greek translation of Job 9:8. Now, soak this in (pardon the pun)—mere people do not walk on water. According to the Old Testament, the only one who walks on the water is Yahweh, as He treads on the waves. But John tells us that Jesus treads on the waves—He walks on water!

If this were the only Old Testament allusion in this passage, we could still say that it is a powerful witness to Jesus's divine identity and therefore worthy of being the fifth of the seven signs of John's gospel. However, there is a second element that alludes to the Old Testament. The disciples were undoubtedly scared; John tells us they were "afraid" (6:19). In our day there are many tales of strange things inhabiting the ocean depths, and in Jesus's day as well the water was perceived as a place of evil where chaos ruled. So this mystique undoubtedly contributed to the disciples' fear that was assuredly compounded when they saw Jesus walking on the water. But when Jesus sought to quell their fears, He told them, "It is I; do not be afraid" (6:20). The Greek literally states, "*Ego eimi*" (I am). In fact, the Greek translation of the Old Testament uses these words to translate from Hebrew God's name when He revealed it to Moses from the burning bush. In John 6:20, Jesus uses the name that Yahweh revealed to Moses: "And God said to Moses, 'I AM WHO I AM [*ego eimi*]'" (Ex. 3:14).

Jesus's walking on the water and His identification of Himself as I AM bring other Old Testament passages to mind:

> The waters saw You, O God;
> The waters saw You, they were afraid;
> The depths also trembled....
> Your way was in the sea,
> Your path in the great waters,
> And Your footsteps were not known. (Ps. 77:16, 19)

Additionally, Jesus tells His disciples, "Do not be afraid" (John 6:20), and these were words that Yahweh frequently said to His Old Testament people, especially as they were on the threshold of the Promised Land (Deut. 1:21, 29; 20:1, 3). Recall Yahweh's words to Joshua: "Have

I not commanded you? Be strong and of good courage; do not be afraid, nor be dismayed, for the LORD your God is with you wherever you go" (Josh. 1:9).

Clearly these Old Testament passages point to Jesus as He tells His disciples, "Fear not, I AM. I alone tread on the waves. Look to Me by faith alone and trust that I will care and provide for you. I will get you to your final destination." John presses his point—namely, that Christ would get the disciples safely to their destination—by making one last Old Testament allusion. John tells us, "Then they willingly received Him into the boat, and immediately the boat was at the land where they were going" (6:21). There is undoubtedly an element of the miraculous here, as once Jesus enters the boat they immediately arrive at their destination. But these words and actions evoke Psalm 107:28–30:

> Then they cry out to the LORD in their trouble,
> And He brings them out of their distresses.
> He calms the storm,
> So that its waves are still.
> Then they are glad because they are quiet;
> So He guides them to their desired haven.

John wanted his readers to think back to passages such as this psalm and recognize that Jesus is the great I AM. The disciples cried out, and Yahweh in the flesh answered their prayers: He stilled the storm and brought them safely to their destination.

Praise Jesus, the Great I AM

As we reflect on this passage, especially against its Old Testament background, it is abundantly clear why this is the fifth of Jesus's seven signs. From all external appearances, Jesus seems to be an ordinary man, but as these miraculous signs begin to accumulate, the average first-century Jew begins to see who He claims to be and truly is. Here is Jesus doing what only Yahweh is capable of doing— walking on the water—and then identifying Himself as the great I AM, who calmed the waters and brought the disciples safely to their destination. Jesus did all this while wearing His coat of many colors, which was sewn together with a patchwork of beautiful Old Testament echoes and allusions. He confirms by His words and deeds that the Old Testament does speak of Him. In short, Jesus is the fulfillment of the Old Testament. How, then, should we respond to this passage?

We get a clue from Psalm 107:31–32, which explains what we are to do after Jesus has calmed our storms and guided us to the desired destination:

> Oh, that men would give thanks to the LORD
>   for His goodness,
> And for His wonderful works to the children
>   of men!
> Let them exalt Him also in the assembly of
>   the people,
> And praise Him in the company of the elders.

When Yahweh calmed the storm, the people responded with thanksgiving and praise. This, I suspect, was the reaction of the disciples after being out on the storm-tossed sea, drenched in water as the waves pounded their small boat and feeling suffocated by the darkness and waves. The contrast of the calm sea and the instantaneous safe arrival on the shore at their destination undoubtedly caused them to be filled with praise and thanksgiving to Jesus.

This should be our response in the light of who Jesus is and what He has done. How often do we praise Christ simply for who He is? How much time do we give to the adoration and praise of our Lord and Savior? Do we praise Him because He is the King of kings and Lord of lords? Do we recognize that He alone is God, that He is self-existent, righteous, holy, powerful, and all knowing? Certainly this passage sets before us the identity of who Jesus is—God in the flesh. However, when we praise Christ for who He is, we should inevitably contemplate what He has done and, more specifically, what He has done for us. Jesus did not perform this sign just to tell His disciples and the church who He is but also to tell them and us what He has done. He alone is God in the flesh who can calm the stormy, chaotic sea and bring His people safely to their destination.

The intent, then, is to show that Jesus will deliver His people from the chaos of their sin and bring them to their destination—the new heavens and new earth and eternal life. As we contemplate how Christ brings this about, we are led through, not around, the cross and are confronted with our sin and inability. As we meditate on who Christ is and what He has done, we must therefore confess and repent of our sinfulness, our lack of praise for Christ, and our doubts about what He has done for us. How often in prayer are we concerned only with bringing our needs

to Christ—giving Him our wish list? This is not to say
that our desires are wrong, though at times they certainly
can be, but there ought to be adoration and praise in our
prayers for who Christ is.

If poets and lyricists have sung the praises of beautiful
sunsets or the loveliness of another person, should not we
who have been delivered from our sin be filled with praise
and adoration for Christ? When we pray, we ought to look
to passages such as John 6:16–21 and praise Christ for His
power to tread on the sea, for His power over the creation—whether the wind or the waves—and because He
is Yahweh, God in the flesh. Moreover, we should read a
passage such as this and see it as a signpost to the certainty
and faithfulness of Christ's great work of redemption.
Have we ever doubted Christ's faithfulness? Have we
ever allowed the circumstances or trials of life to drown
us in feelings of hopelessness or despair? In the face of
such things, whether frustrations, illnesses, persecutions,
or struggles, remember that Christ has not abandoned us.
Not only has He delivered us from the miry depths of sin
and death, but He also watches over us every step of the
way so that He will most assuredly bring us to our destination. Christ will plant our feet on the shore of the new
heavens and new earth.

Conclusion

Therefore, praise Christ for who He is and what He has
done. May the words of the psalmist be on our lips:

Oh, that men would give thanks to the LORD
    for His goodness,

And for His wonderful works to the children
  of men!
Let them exalt Him also in the assembly of
  the people,
And praise Him in the company of the elders.
  (Ps. 107:31–32)

Praise Jesus, the great I AM!

▶ **Questions for Further Study**

    1. According to the Old Testament, who is the only one who treads on the waves?

    2. Why is it significant that Jesus says, "I AM; do not be afraid," as He walks on the water?

    3. In what way are the events of John 6:16–21 connected to Psalm 107?

CHAPTER 2

The Bread of Life
John 6:22–59

> *I am the bread of life.... I am the living bread*
> *which came down from heaven.*
> —JOHN 6:48, 51

What do you see when you look at Christ? Some people see only a moral teacher, but some see the Son of God in the flesh. Is Christ merely a good teacher who passes on life principles, or is He the Son of God who gives eternal life to those who believe in Him? The answers to these questions lie in John 6:22–59, where Jesus makes the claim to be the bread of life. When Jesus says, "I am the bread of life," He unfurls His Old Testament coat to show that He indeed is the long-awaited fulfillment of God's covenant promises.

The crowd that followed Him, however, was not thinking with their hearts but with their stomachs. They knew that Jesus had just miraculously fed them, and they wanted more. Rather than give them more bread, Jesus identified their real need—the bread of life that would bring them salvation—indeed, He pointed to His identity as the Messiah and Savior. But many in the crowd were unwilling to receive Jesus's message. They wanted food in their bellies rather than Christ in their hearts. Jesus challenged them with the truth of the gospel—He pushed past their appetites and showed them what they truly needed, and to this day His words continue to ring out. Will we seek Christ for the forgiveness of our sins and eternal life? Or will we look for poor substitutes, pursuing Christ for other reasons that fall short of the kingdom of God—for financial, material, or personal gain? Christ clearly reveals Himself as the only means by which we can be saved—He is the bread of life.

Looking for Food

The passage begins by recounting the events the day after Jesus walked on the water. The crowds that follow Jesus wake up and look for Him, but they cannot find Him. Driven by hunger covered by a thin veil of piety, they conduct an investigation and determine where Jesus has gone. The crowd does not fool Jesus—He knows that they want food and not His instruction, not the words of life: "Jesus answered them and said, 'Most assuredly, I say to you, you seek Me, not because you saw the signs, but because you ate of the loaves and were filled'" (John 6:26). They want more bread. Jesus, however, tells them, "Do not labor for the food which perishes, but for the food which endures to everlasting life." Jesus tells them that He, the Son of Man, will give them this bread (6:27).

Notice, though, that Jesus calls Himself the Son of Man rather than the Messiah. "Son of Man" is just as important a title because it connects Jesus to Adam, the first son of man, and identifies Jesus as the one who would restore God's rule to the creation. This title was less politically charged than "Messiah," which invoked images of a warrior who would run off Israel's enemies (see, e.g., Psalm 2). Christ's choice of titles also suggests that the crowds were looking for more than food: they wanted an earthly king, someone who would throw off the yoke of Roman oppression and restore Israel's freedom. The people want full bellies and freedom from Rome, but Jesus offers something entirely different.

The crowd bristles at Jesus's words and asks Him what they must do to receive eternal life, to which Jesus responds: "This is the work of God, that you believe in Him whom He sent" (6:29). The crowd understands Jesus's statement—that He is really saying, "Believe in Me." So the crowd responds to Jesus by saying, "Give us a reason that we should believe in You." This is why they ask for a sign: "What sign will You perform then, that we may see it and believe You?" (6:30). The crowd's request is thick with irony and burdened by disbelief. Jesus had just miraculously fed them, yet they ask Him what sign He would perform. In addition, they invoke the name of Moses and his miraculous feeding of Israel in the wilderness. They are comparing Jesus to Moses and trying to goad Him into providing more food. They are, in effect, saying, "Moses was a great leader and He fed the people, so if you want to be a great leader, You need to feed us." The crowd wants food, but Jesus points to their need for faith in Him, and they meet His words with more verbal fencing.

Jesus reminds the crowd that Moses did not feed Israel, but that God, His heavenly Father, fed them. Moreover, the bread that God gave them was temporal and perishable—the wilderness generation had died. Jesus contrasts the heavenly manna with the bread He would give them, bread that would bring them eternal life. The crowd eagerly responds, "Lord, give us this bread always" (6:34). The crowd probably was still motivated by their growling stomachs rather than the hunger and thirst for righteousness that Christ spoke of in His Sermon on the Mount (Matt. 5:6). Unmoved by their hunger, Jesus points them to the true manna from heaven: "I am the bread of life. He who comes to Me shall never hunger, and he who believes in Me shall never thirst" (John 6:35).

Manna from Heaven

Powerfully alluding to Israel's Old Testament wanderings, Jesus shows how Moses wrote about Him (John 5:46). He connects God's giving Israel manna from heaven with His incarnation and condescension to man. When God rained bread on a rebellious people, He was giving not only an act of kindness and grace but also a shadowy portrait of sending His Son to sinful humanity that they might eat of this heavenly bread and live forever. There is a big difference between Israel's manna and Jesus, the bread of life. Christ's point is that the people must believe in Him—trusting in Jesus, not consuming bread, brings eternal life. In the words of Augustine, "If you have believed, you have eaten."[1]

As easy as this is for us to understand, the statement would have been repulsive to many people in the crowd. Jesus has identified Himself as the Son of God, the manna come down from heaven. But rather than try to soften the

---

1. Augustine, *Tractates on the Gospel of John*, Fathers of the Church, vol. 88 (Washington, D.C.: Catholic University of America Press, 1993), tractate 25.12.

blow of the truth, Jesus adorns His bread from heaven with a garnish of divine sovereignty: "But I said to you that you have seen Me and yet do not believe. All that the Father gives Me will come to Me, and the one who comes to Me I will by no means cast out" (6:36–37).

Jesus says that the reason they have not believed in Him is because the Father has not granted it to them. The Father must enable a person to believe through the work of the Holy Spirit, who opens our eyes, ears, and minds to accept and believe in the gospel of Christ and in this way receive eternal life. The crowd did not take kindly to what Jesus was saying. They were upset that He identified Himself as the bread that had come down from heaven (6:41). They asked themselves, "Is not this Jesus, the son of Joseph, whose father and mother we know?" (6:42). Many in the crowd looked on this young man and saw only someone ordinary—a carpenter's son—not God incarnate. And like their forefathers of old, the crowd began to grumble. They were also offended because Jesus had just told them they were incapable of consuming this heavenly meal. Undaunted by their grumbling and complaining, Jesus presses His point again: "Do not murmur among yourselves. No one can come to Me unless the Father who sent Me draws him; and I will raise him up at the last day" (6:43–44). We should realize that Jesus is not saying anything new. The idea that God must enable a person to believe goes back to the earliest portions of the Scriptures.

Think, for example, of Moses's words to Israel just before they entered the Promised Land: "Therefore circumcise the foreskin of your heart, and be stiff-necked no longer" (Deut. 10:16). The Lord knew that His people would not and could not circumcise their hearts. To put it in Pauline terms, they were dead in their sins and trespasses. What do dead people do? Nothing. This is why even in the context of Deuteronomy the command to circumcise their hearts became a promise: "And the LORD your God will circumcise your heart and the heart of your descendants, to love the LORD your God with all your heart and with all your soul, that you may live" (Deut. 30:6). John has echoed this theme from the outset of his gospel:

> He came to His own, and His own did not receive Him. But as many as received Him, to them He gave the right to become children of God, to those who believe in His name: who were born, not of blood, nor of the will of the flesh, nor of the will of man, but God. (1:11–13)

> Most assuredly, I say to you, unless one is born again, he cannot see the kingdom of God. (3:3)

> Most assuredly, I say to you, unless one is born of water and the Spirit, he cannot enter the kingdom of God. (3:5)

In John 6:45, Jesus reinforces His claim by appealing to Isaiah 54:13, which says that God Himself would teach His people and bring them to the Son. At this point in the exchange between Jesus and the crowd, we might think that He would in some way try to soften the impact of this theological truth, but rather than soften the blow, He sharpens the edge of truth.

Jesus says in verse 51, "I am the living bread which came down from heaven. If anyone eats of this bread, he will live forever; and the bread that I shall give is My flesh, which I shall give for the life of the world." Jesus presses His point by telling them what would undoubtedly be repulsive to any person, but especially to a first-century Jew, given the ceremonial food laws. There is also the distinct possibility that the people thought Jesus was referring to cannibalism. This would certainly explain their reaction to Christ's words. We do see a negative reaction from the crowd in verse 52; they ask, "How can this Man give us His flesh to eat?" Jesus pushes them beyond their limits:

> Most assuredly, I say to you, unless you eat the flesh of the Son of Man and drink His blood, you have no life in you. Whoever eats My flesh and drinks My blood has eternal life, and I will raise him up at the last day. For My flesh is food indeed, and My blood is drink indeed. He who eats My flesh and drinks My blood abides in Me, and I in him. (6:53–56)

This statement would have been especially offensive to Jews because they were forbidden by the ceremonial law to consume blood—especially human blood.

Will We Eat the Manna?

As we reflect on this exchange between Jesus and the crowd, the question naturally arises: Why did Jesus say these things? Why did He force this issue? Why did He not soften the truth to appeal in some way to His audience?

There are two broad answers to these questions. The first answer comes in the nature of man's heart. Given our fallen condition, we live in a state of rebellion and spiritual death concerning the things of God. We must realize that, as Paul tells us in the first chapter of Romans, submitting to God's authority and believing in Christ are not intellectual problems, but chiefly moral ones: "Although they knew God, they did not glorify Him as God, nor were thankful, but became futile in their thoughts, and their foolish hearts were darkened" (Rom. 1:21). Given man's fallen condition, there is no way to soften the truth. You cannot put sugar on the rim of the bitter cup of salvation to make its contents more appealing. The truth in any form will always be offensive to fallen sinners. You cannot bid the world to die and expect a warm reaction.

This is a problem with much of the church these days: it tries to water down the truth in an effort to make it more acceptable to people, but then the people never end up closing the deal. There are likely hundreds of thousands, if not millions, who are in churches who have never heard the offense of the gospel. Why do I say the "offense" of the gospel? Because deep down inside all men hate God; this is what Paul tells us in Romans 3:1–19. People will inevitably react with hostility, therefore, toward the gospel of Christ. Jonathan Edwards once said that it does not matter how God comes to man; unbelievers will always find an excuse to reject Him. If God comes in might, power, and strength, unbelieving man will say, "He is too strong." If he comes in weakness, humility, and love, people will say, "He is too weak." Christ captures something of this observation when he responds to the crowds:

But to what shall I liken this generation? It is like children sitting in the marketplaces and calling to their companions, and saying,

> "We played the flute for you,
>   And you did not dance;
> "We mourned to you,
>   And you did not lament."

For John [the Baptist] came neither eating nor drinking, and they say, "He has a demon." The Son of Man came eating and drinking, and they say, "Look, a glutton and a winebibber, a friend of tax collectors and sinners!" (Matt. 11:16–19)

This is why God must enable people to believe through the work of the Holy Spirit, who removes the heart of stone and gives a heart of flesh. He opens the eyes, ears, and heart to receive the truth so that people will believe in Jesus. This is what ultimately lies behind Jesus's teaching here.

The second answer comes from understanding that Jesus is wrapping Himself in the Old Testament. He was not simply looking for the most insulting way to present the truth. On the contrary, if we listen with the ears of the Old Testament, we realize that Jesus was showing the crowds His coat of many colors. Not only does He identify Himself as the living bread from heaven, but He also implicitly identifies Himself as the sacrifice that gives life. Remember in the Old Testament that sacrifices ceremonially cleansed the Israelites and allowed them to dwell in God's presence. Indeed, some of the sacrifices were supposed to be eaten in the presence of God in celebration and thanksgiving for the redemption that was to come from Him. Jesus was identifying Himself as the fulfillment of those Old Testament sacrifices when He told the people that they had to eat His flesh and drink His blood. Moreover, when Jesus said they had to drink His blood, He undoubtedly intended it as a foil against the Old Testament prohibition against consuming blood—the life of the creature was in the blood (Gen. 9:4). Therefore, it seems that Jesus is saying, "Life is in Me!"

This is how we must see the overall intent of the passage. Jesus is not saying that we must literally consume His flesh and blood in order to have eternal life. Such an interpretation flies in the face of the passage. Rather, the intent of the passage is that the people had to believe in Jesus (emphasis added in the following verses):

- This is the work of God, that you *believe in Him* whom He sent (6:29).

- What sign will You perform then, that we may see it and *believe You* (6:30)?

- But I said to you that you have seen Me and yet *do not believe* (6:36).

- Everyone who sees the Son and *believes in Him* may have everlasting life (6:40).

This especially becomes clear in the parallel statements from verses 40 and 54. Verse 40 mentions believing in Christ to receive eternal life, whereas verse 54 speaks of consuming Christ to receive eternal life: "Whoever eats My flesh and drinks My blood has eternal life, and I will raise him up at the last day." Jesus is saying that He is the sacrifice, and it was by believing in Him that they would receive eternal life.

Quite simply, then, will you believe in Jesus? So often people live their lives in search of different ways to fill their hunger and thirst: they seek contentment in possessions, friendships, family, jobs, drugs, themselves, and anything else they can lay their hands on. Many people even come to Jesus looking for earthly things—the "health and wealth" gospel aptly captures these erroneous motives. People seek to fill the grumbling discontentment in their hearts with material blessings that supposedly come from Jesus. Or, they align themselves with Jesus because they believe He is an icon of morality, a political messiah, or a good teacher. Yet if this passage teaches anything, it is that we have a Jesus-shaped hole in our hearts, and He is the only one who can fill it. As Augustine once wrote, "You stir man to take pleasure in praising you, because you have made us for yourself, and our heart is restless until it rests in you."[2]

Correlatively, the same misguided spiritual eating habits mark the church—those who truly trust in Jesus, who have tasted the bread from heaven and have received the gift of eternal life through faith alone in Him by God's grace alone. As we wander in the wilderness of this world, we encounter obstacles and trials and are tempted to return to the meat, leeks, and vegetables of Egypt. Or, as we pilgrim through the wilderness, we stop along the

---

2. Augustine, *Confessions*, trans. Henry Chadwick (Oxford: Oxford University Press, 1991), 1.1.

way and fill our stomachs with all the food that the world has to offer. By the time we come to the Lord's Table to feast on the manna from heaven, our bellies are full, and we do not hunger and thirst for righteousness. We have consumed our share of the world's delicacies and have no appetite for Christ.

Quite simply, Christ calls you to look to Him by faith alone and recognize that you can do this by God's grace alone. Feed on Christ—turn away from the table of the world and feast on the manna from heaven. Break open the bread of life and daily feed your soul through the reading of God's Word. Consume the bread of life as you meditate on Christ's Word in prayer. Join with God's pilgrim people every Lord's Day and rejoice in the magnificent banquet that God has set before you in the presence of your enemies. In the midst of this wasteland of the world, God has rained Christ down from heaven, and streams of living water flow from beneath the threshold of the heavenly temple to assuage your hunger and thirst. Look on and taste the word of Christ in the sacraments, God's visible words by which He heralds the gospel. In all of these things, believe, and you have eaten.

Conclusion

Faith is the mouth of the soul, and we must look to Jesus by a God-given faith that we may have eternal life. Not only do we need to look by faith to Jesus for the initial point of our salvation, but indeed throughout our entire lives. Give thanks that God has opened your eyes to see the truth of the gospel and to repent of your sin. Repent of your sin even now. Repent of your unbelief. Rejoice that

Christ has come, lived, died, been raised, and ascended to the right hand of the Father that we might have life. Look therefore by faith on Jesus and be filled with the hope of eternal life.

▶ **Questions for Further Study**

    1. Why did the crowds seek Christ?

    2. What Old Testament event did Christ allude to when He identified Himself as the manna from heaven?

    3. How did Augustine characterize eating the manna from heaven?

    4. Is the main point of the text eating or believing? Explain your answer.

CHAPTER 3

The Light of the World
John 8:12–59

*Jesus spoke to them again, saying, "I am the light
of the world. He who follows Me shall not walk
in darkness, but have the light of life."* —JOHN 8:12

In Mark Twain's story *Adventures of Tom Sawyer*, Tom Sawyer and Becky Thatcher join their classmates for a game
of hide-and-seek in a cave, but eventually they wander off
the marked path and get lost. They walk around in the
earthen dungeon for days and slowly begin to lose hope as
their flickering candle eventually goes out and leaves them
in complete darkness. They can see nothing, not even
their hands held up close to their faces. They try to crawl
about but are fearful that they might fall down a massive
hole or crack. Tom is finally able to catch a glimpse of
daylight through a crevice, makes his way back to Becky,
and leads her out of the cave into the bright light of day.
As Tom and Becky's experience shows, even the smallest
glimmer of light can be a source of hope, guidance, and
direction in the midst of darkness.

It would have been a strange plot twist if Tom, seeing
the glimmer of light, had retreated back into the darkness rather than follow it to safety. But John 8 describes a

situation where that is exactly what happened. People who were groping about in darkness retreated further into it when they were given the opportunity to come into the light. We see this in the crowd's reaction to Christ's teaching when He claims to be the light of the world. In the dark world, Jesus is ultimately the only light by which we can see, but rather than run to the light, like Tom Sawyer did, some retreat into the darkness.

At the Feast of Tabernacles, a celebration that recalled Israel's wilderness wanderings and God's provision for them during that time, Jesus makes one of His famous "I am" statements: "I am the light of the world" (John 8:12). In the middle of this festival, Jesus once again points to Old Testament prophecies, images, and themes. He tells the crowds that He is the only source of light in the morally dark world. As the people around him grope in their spiritual darkness, Jesus shines His light on them. He takes the gospel and shines its white-hot light immediately in the crowd's eyes. But rather than fall on their faces and repent, the crowd instead retreats to the shadows and darkness.

We must understand Jesus's claims and what He means when He says that He is the light of the world. Moreover, we must pray that we would flee the darkness rather than the light. In order to understand the significance of this passage, we will examine Christ's claims that He is the light of the world and His two claims to the divine name I AM. We want to understand Christ's claims, but equally important is the crowd's response. Instead of falling to their faces, they pick up stones to execute Jesus. Only by God's grace will we drop our stones and fall on Jesus, the chief cornerstone and stumbling stone of offense, and cry out for God's mercy that He does not fall on us in judgment.

I Am the Light of the World

We encounter Jesus on the last day of the Feast of Tabernacles. Jewish literature indicates that on the evening of the last day of the feast, the temple officials lit four large lamps in the temple courts. People celebrated and men danced throughout the night, holding burning torches in their hands while singing praises to the Lord. Early sources testify that the light from the temple would bathe the surrounding city, which was enveloped in darkness. Many in the crowd undoubtedly lost themselves in the gaiety of the celebrations, but others likely traveled back in time and, through the Old Testament Scriptures, recalled Israel's wanderings in the wilderness. They remembered the massive pillar of fire that jutted into the dark sky, leading Israel through the wilderness. In the midst of this Old Testament–charged night air, Jesus declares to the people: "I am the light of the world. He who follows Me shall not walk in darkness, but have the light of life" (John 8:12).

During the feast the people would conduct a water-drawing ceremony that celebrated God's provision of water for the people in the wilderness. At that ceremony Jesus told the people that He would give anyone who believed in Him living water (John 7:37–39). The context for this ceremony is the exodus, and particularly God's presence in the pillar of fire by night to lead the Israelites through the wilderness. Jesus once again dons His coat of Old Testament colors and informs the crowds that He is the light of the world, and that anyone who follows Him will receive the light of life. When we consider other statements in the Old Testament concerning God and light, we see that Jesus is saying He is God: "The LORD is my light and my salvation; whom shall I fear?" (Ps. 27:1). The psalmist famously writes, "Your word is a lamp to my feet and a light to my path" (119:105).

Given these Old Testament statements, Jesus is saying that He is the Word incarnate, God in the flesh, and that anyone who believes in Him will have eternal life. He identifies Himself with Yahweh, the pillar of fire that led Israel through the nighttime wilderness. Jesus does not leave the veil over His identity, however, but states clearly that He is God in the flesh when He says that He is the light of the world. It is important to note that Jesus does not merely say, "I am the light of Israel," as true as that would be. Rather, He says quite boldly, "I am the light of the *world*" (John 8:12, emphasis added). In other words, Jesus does not merely bring the light of redemption to His fellow Jews, but to anyone, Jew or Gentile, who believes in Him.

I AM, I AM

To make His point even clearer, Jesus makes His first explicit claim to be the great I AM in the flesh. He tells the crowds: "I said to you that you will die in your sins; for if you do not believe that *I am*...you will die in your sins" (8:24, emphasis added). Again, just as in John 6:20, Jesus invokes the Greek form of I AM (*ego eimi*). This statement might not seem all that earth shattering, especially for those who have repeatedly heard this message throughout their lives in the preaching of the gospel. However, against the backdrop of the Old Testament, this statement takes on a much greater significance. Consider the words of Isaiah the prophet:

> Who has performed and done it,
> Calling the generations from the beginning?
> "I, the LORD, am the first;
> And with the last I am He [the Septuagint, the
> Greek translation of the Old Testament, has 'I
> AM']." (Isa. 41:4)

Here Jesus makes His first claim to be the great I AM. This is no minor statement to make. Isaiah explains what would happen to anyone who claimed to be like God—that is, self-sufficient:

> Therefore hear this now, you who are given
>   to pleasures,
> Who dwell securely,
> Who say in your heart, "I am, and there is no
>   one else besides me;
> I shall not sit as a widow,
> Nor shall I know the loss of children";
> But these two things shall come to you
> In a moment, in one day:
> The loss of children, and widowhood.
> They shall come upon you in their fullness
> Because of the multitude of your sorceries,
> For the great abundance of your enchantments.
>   (Isa. 47:8–9)

The prophet Zephaniah offers a similar warning:

This is the rejoicing city
That dwelt securely,
That said in her heart,
  "I am it, and there is none besides me."
How has she become a desolation,
A place for beasts to lie down! (2:15)

So if Jesus was making a false claim, He was, in effect, calling a curse upon Himself.

Instead of withdrawing the claim, He adds a second: "When you lift up the Son of Man, then you will know that *I am* . . . and that I do nothing of Myself; but as My Father taught Me, I speak these things. And He who sent Me is with Me. The Father has not left Me alone, for I always do those things that please Him" (John 8:28–29, emphasis added). Jesus refers to His crucifixion when He speaks of lifting up the Son of Man, but He is also referring to His resurrection and exaltation at the right hand of the Father. When He is lifted up and exalted, then they will know that He is the great I AM. But notice an important point here: He claims to be the great I AM, God in the flesh, but He is also willing to obey the will of His heavenly Father, even to the point of death, death on the cross. Christ's obedience stands in stark contrast to the disobedience of the religious leaders and many of the Jews in the crowd.

The Reaction

Many in the crowd, especially the religious leaders, are hostile to what Jesus is saying. Their hostility to Christ leaps off the page in the events recounted in John 7. Far from abating, their anger and hatred reach high tide here in John 8. In response to Christ's claim that He is the light of the world, they interrogate Him about His statement that He is bearing witness to Himself. Jesus tells them that He not only testified but that His Father also testified concerning His identity. Notice the response in verse 19: "Then they said to Him, 'Where is Your Father?'" This is no ordinary question. The crowd was not simply saying, "You're talking about your father—where is he?" Rather, they ask a loaded question, "Where *is* your father?" In other words, they are aware of the rumors surrounding Jesus's birth (that He was born of a virgin and hence had no earthly father) and are therefore implying that He is an illegitimate child.

The crowd's hostility becomes even more pointed, and they accuse Him of being demon possessed and hurl the stone of a racial epithet at him: "Do we not say rightly that You are a Samaritan and have a demon?" (8:48). They accuse Jesus of being a Samaritan, invoking an age-old rivalry between the Jews and the Samaritans. As in our day, if you want to insult someone, you question his birth or ridicule his race. The Jews, for example, said that the Samaritans were the offspring of Cain. Some in the crowd were therefore questioning Jesus's paternity. But if that were not enough, they also accused Him of being demon possessed.

Some of the Jews in the crowd cast aspersions on Jesus's paternity and in contrast put forward their own paternal heritage by claiming to be descendants of Abraham: "We are Abraham's descendants, and have never been in bondage to anyone. How can You say, 'You will be

made free'" (8:33)? They offer this statement in response
to Jesus's claim that they are enslaved. Their assertion is
arrogant, prideful, and blind to the truth. Not only are
they blind to who Jesus is and, in turn, to who His Father
is, but they also deny that they are doubly enslaved. The
slavery that Jesus is talking about is their enslavement to
the power of Satan, sin, and death. This is evident because
Jesus tells them quite clearly: "You are of your father the
devil, and the desires of your father you want to do. He
was a murderer from the beginning, and does not stand
in the truth, because there is no truth in him. When he
speaks a lie, he speaks from his own resources, for he is
a liar and the father of it" (8:44). The crowds were not
demon possessed, but they were definitely following their
father, Satan, by hurling the stones of accusations, insults,
and hatred at Jesus.

But on top of their spiritual slavery, they were also
under the rule of the Romans! They were blind to their
sin and to their present bondage to Rome. They must
have simply been cross-eyed with hatred. Jesus shines
the light of truth on them, and they scurry off to the
recesses of their hearts, where they find comfort and sol-
ace in the darkness. And from their fortresses of darkness,
they hurl another stone of insult: "Abraham is our father"
(8:39). And so Jesus responds to their insults and claims
of superiority by shining more light on their sin-darkened
hearts: "If you were Abraham's children, you would do
the works of Abraham. But now you seek to kill Me, a
Man who has told you the truth which I heard from God.
Abraham did not do this" (8:39–40). Jesus quite pointedly
shows them that if they truly were sons of Abraham, they

would believe in Him. Instead, they are offspring of their father Satan.

I AM Thrice

So far, Jesus has made one indirect claim to be God when He said that He is the light of the world. He has also made two direct claims to deity. Conversely, the crowd has twice rejected Christ's claims. How does Christ finally respond? He makes a third crystal-clear statement regarding His identity. Jesus tells the unbelieving crowds once again that if they believe in Him, they will never see death (8:52). This was the final straw for many in the crowd, who object, "Abraham is dead" (8:52)! "Are You greater than our father Abraham, who is dead? And the prophets are dead. Who do You make Yourself out to be?" (8:53). The crowd rains down their verbal stones on Christ, to which Jesus responds:

> If I honor Myself, My honor is nothing. It is My Father who honors Me, of whom you say that He is your God. Yet you have not known Him, but I know Him. And if I say, "I do not know Him," I shall be a liar like you; but I do know Him and keep His word. Your father Abraham rejoiced to see My day, and he saw it and was glad. (8:54–56)

Jesus tells the crowd that Abraham, the great patriarch, looked for Jesus's day—which is a stunning statement. It tells us that the patriarchs were not looking to God generically or simply to a bald promise of redemption, but specifically to Jesus, the Messiah, to save them—God in the flesh.

At this statement the people in the crowd balk. How could Jesus know Abraham? Here Jesus makes His third and most explicit claim to deity: "Most assuredly, I say to you, before Abraham was, I AM" (8:58). This time the crowd knows specifically what Jesus is saying, and they drop their verbal stones and pick up rocks to kill Him. John tells us that Jesus hid Himself, however, and went out of the temple. Jesus was not running from the crowds, fearing for His life. After all, He had just claimed to be the great I AM. Rather, if we consider Jesus's three explicit claims to be the great I AM and remember that the place of the conversation was in the temple precincts, there is something far more ominous in His disappearance. Jesus's action is one of judgment. Think of it: Jesus is God in the flesh tabernacled in Israel's midst—indeed, He is present in the temple, His earthly dwelling place. But now He leaves His temple, abandoning it. In the language of the Old Testament, God hid His face—Christ's absence meant the presence of judgment (Deut. 32:20). The rocks the crowd clenched in their angry fists would rebound on their own heads as Jesus Christ, the stone of stumbling and rock of offense, would instead fall on them.

Conclusion

As those who believe in Christ, we are dumbfounded at the crowd's response. How can they pick up stones to try to kill the great I AM? Why would they want to kill God in the flesh? The answer is a simple one—God in Christ shined His light on them and at the same time revealed their sinfulness. Or, in Christ's words: "The light has come into the world, and men loved darkness rather than light, because their deeds were evil" (John 3:19). He told them the truth—they were in bondage to their father Satan. He told them that the only way they could be saved and freed from this bondage was to believe in Him. They could not save themselves. Moreover, as we can clearly see, they did not want to save themselves.

The only reason we can read this passage and be dumbfounded by the crowd's response is because Jesus, the great I AM, has saved us. He has broken the bonds of Satan, sin, and death; opened our eyes that we might see Him for who He is; and opened our hearts that we would trust and believe in His life, death, resurrection, and ascension. As we recognize the blindness of the people, we should be filled with joy and thanksgiving that we can see and believe. We should be filled with joy and praise for the great I AM who has come to save us from our sins. Apart from God's mercy and grace in Christ applied by the Holy Spirit, we too would take rocks in hand and try to kill God incarnate. We too would look into the face of the Son of God and insult Him. Yet, as John elsewhere has said, "Behold what manner of love the Father has bestowed on us, that we should be called children of God!" (1 John 3:1).

▶ **Questions for Further Study**

1. What Old Testament festival were the people celebrating? What was its significance?

2. How many times in John 8 does Jesus invoke the divine name I AM?

3. Why does Jesus tell the crowds, "Before Abraham was, I AM"?

CHAPTER 4

The Door and the Good Shepherd

John 10:1–21

> *Jesus said to them again, "I am the door of the sheep.... I am the good shepherd. The good shepherd gives His life for the sheep.*
>
> —JOHN 10: 7, 11

In the ancient world, kings used the common metaphor of a shepherd to describe their relationship to their subjects. Sheep are totally dependent on a shepherd to lead and guide them, and they rely on their shepherd to protect them. Shamash, the Mesopotamian sun god, was described as the shepherd of all that was beneath him. The Egyptian sun god, Amon, is described as a shepherd who provides food for his suffering people.[1] In the seventh century BC, Neo-Assyrian king Ashurbanipal covered the walls of his palace in Nineveh with images of him slaying lions in defense of his people.[2] In short, the king-as-shepherd was powerful, paternal, and beneficent. We can see, then, that because the people of the ancient world

---

1. "Common Metaphors for God," in *The IVP Bible Background Commentary*, ed. John H. Walton, Victor H. Matthews, and Mark W. Chavalas (Downers Grove, Ill.: InterVarsity, 2014), 515.

2. Fred Kleiner, *Gardner's Art Through the Ages: A Global History*, 14th ed. (Boston: Wadsworth, 2013), 48.

were familiar with this metaphor, Christ appeals to it and
uses it to describe His own relationship with His subjects.
As the King of kings and Lord of lords, Jesus wants His
people to know that He is the good shepherd. But in a
counterintuitive move, He turns the shepherd metaphor
on its head.

Jesus is unique as the good shepherd—He says that
He lays His life down for the sheep. Unlike the kings of
the ancient Near East, Jesus serves as a sacrifice for His
people. To understand the significance of Christ's claim
"I am the good shepherd," as well as its correlative claim
"I am the door," we must explore three things. First, we
must understand the immediate context of Christ's claims.
Why does He raise the subject of shepherds? Why does
Christ's conflict with the religious leaders lead to His discourse about being the good shepherd? Second, how does
Jesus describe Himself as the good shepherd? What does
it mean that He is the door? What is the significance of
His willingness to lay down His life for His sheep? Finally,
how should the sheep live in light of the life-giving work
of the good shepherd?

Israel's Bad Shepherds

What precipitated Christ's discourse on the good shepherd? The immediate context provides an answer. In
John 9 the religious leaders criticize Jesus because He had
healed a man born blind. They are offended not simply
because Jesus healed the man, but because He had performed this miracle on the Sabbath. The religious leaders
looked past the miracle in their effort to harangue Jesus
over His perceived violation of the law. Their blindness

to the miracle signals that a conflict will ensue. The blind man subsequently has two encounters with the religious leaders, who question him over what had happened to him in his two meetings with Jesus. The chapter ends on both a negative and a positive note.

Negatively, the man is excommunicated from the synagogue for his stated belief in Jesus. He defends Jesus and rebukes the religious leaders. Here is a simple, uneducated man who is schooling the religious leaders on who Jesus is. Positively, Jesus encounters the man He had healed and informs him that He is the Son of Man, the one who would restore His Father's kingdom to the creation. In effect, Jesus is Israel's king. The formerly blind man embraces Jesus as his king, the Messiah, and places his faith in Him, while the religious leaders look into the face of God and reject His claims to rightly rule over Israel. They refuse to believe in Jesus and to recognize who He truly is. Also, they are leading the people astray—away from Israel's king and into rebellion.

This turn of events provokes Jesus's good shepherd discourse, which He begins by showing how Israel's leaders have failed in their responsibilities. Jesus, therefore, begins by describing the nature of a true shepherd. At first glance this might seem like a non sequitur. Why would Jesus bring up the imagery of a shepherd just as He has declared the religious leaders blind? The answer comes from the Old Testament, as does much of the imagery connected with this passage. The prophet Ezekiel described the religious leaders in his own day in the following manner:

Son of man, prophesy against the shepherds of
Israel, prophesy and say to them, "Thus says the
Lord GOD to the shepherds: 'Woe to the shepherds of Israel who feed themselves! Should not
the shepherds feed the flocks? You eat the fat and
clothe yourselves with the wool; you slaughter
the fatlings, but you do not feed the flock. The
weak you have not strengthened, nor have you
healed those who were sick, nor bound up the
broken, nor brought back what was driven away,
nor sought what was lost; but with force and cru-
elty you have ruled them. So they were scattered
because there was no shepherd; and they became
food for all the beasts of the field when they were
scattered. My sheep wandered through all the
mountains, and on every high hill; yes, My flock
was scattered over the whole face of the earth,
and no one was seeking or searching for them.'"
(Ezek. 34:2–6)

Rather than leading the sheep of Israel to the one true
shepherd, the religious leaders are scattering them to serve
their own selfish interests. Selfishness and poor leader-
ship provoke Jesus to use the imagery of a shepherd. Why
are the religious leaders responding in this way? They are
scattering the sheep because Jesus challenges their authority and shines the light of truth on their self-serving ways.
The leaders are devouring the sheep and driving them
over the precipice of rebellion against God.

I Am the Good Shepherd

Contrasting Himself with the self-serving shepherds of Israel, Jesus tells the crowds that He is not a thief or a robber, one who would come in to steal sheep (John 10:1–2). Some of the imagery that Jesus uses is perhaps unfamiliar to those who live in the West. Typically, in the West shepherds drive sheep—they push them along with a sheepdog nipping at their heels. In the Middle East, however, shepherds do not drive the sheep; they lead them—they use specific calls by which the sheep recognize their shepherd and follow him wherever he goes. Again, though, we should drive further back into the Old Testament to grasp the deeper significance of what Jesus is saying. The prophet Ezekiel provides the Old Testament backdrop to Christ's statements:

> For thus says the Lord GOD: "Indeed I Myself will search for My sheep and seek them out. As a shepherd seeks out his flock on the day he is among his scattered sheep, so will I seek out My sheep and deliver them from all the places where they were scattered on a cloudy and dark day. And I will bring them out from the peoples and gather them from the countries, and will bring them to their own land; I will feed them on the mountains of Israel, in the valleys and in all the inhabited places of the country. I will feed them in good pasture, and their fold shall be on the high mountains of Israel. There they shall lie down in a good fold and feed in rich pasture on the mountains of Israel. I will feed My flock, and I will make them

lie down," says the Lord GOD. "I will seek what
was lost and bring back what was driven away,
bind up the broken and strengthen what was sick;
but I will destroy the fat and the strong, and feed
them in judgment." (Ezek. 34:11–16)

Against this backdrop, Christ is leading up to the
claim that *He* is God in the flesh—Yahweh—who promised that He would personally shepherd the sheep of
Israel. He would provide for them, He would lead them,
He would seek the lost, He would strengthen the weak,
and He would protect them from their enemies and judge
the wicked.

Ezekiel's prophecy has deeper roots in the Old Testament, in the days of Israel's exodus. Moses prophesied:
"Let the LORD, the God of the spirits of all flesh, set a
man over the congregation, who may go out before them
and go in before them, who may lead them out and bring
them in, that the congregation of the LORD may not be like
sheep which have no shepherd" (Num. 27:16–17). Moses
told the people that someday Yahweh would appoint one
man who would shepherd them, a man anointed by the
Spirit. Jesus is this one man.

Hence, Jesus once again puts on His Old Testament
coat of many colors and identifies Himself as Israel's true
shepherd. He says that the sheep hear His voice, and He
calls them. Jesus even says that He calls them "by name
and leads them out" (10:3). He asserts that His sheep will
follow Him, and not a stranger (10:4–5). This is certainly
evident from the previous chapter, where the formerly
blind man would not follow the religious leaders, but only

Jesus. John tells us in verse 6, however, that the people in the crowd did not understand what Jesus was saying. So Jesus continues to press the imagery and identifies Himself as the door for the sheep. In so doing, He has some sharp words of condemnation for the religious leaders.

Jesus says, "I am the door. If anyone enters by Me, he will be saved, and will go in and out and find pasture. The thief does not come except to steal, and to kill, and to destroy. I have come that they may have life, and that they may have it more abundantly" (10:9–10). Notice the stark contrast between Jesus and the religious leaders: they are interested only in stealing, killing, and destroying, but Jesus has come to save sheep. Moreover, not only does He save the sheep as the door by which they must enter in order to be saved, but He also gives His life for the sheep: "I am the good shepherd. The good shepherd gives His life for the sheep. But a hireling, he who is not the shepherd, one who does not own the sheep, sees the wolf coming and leaves the sheep and flees; and the wolf catches the sheep and scatters them. The hireling flees because he is a hireling and does not care about the sheep" (10:11–13). Unlike the religious leaders who were willing to kill Jesus in the effort to protect their own place of authority, He was willing to lay down His life for the sheep. We should realize that Jesus is not saying He would die a martyr's death at the hand of His persecutors but that He is genuinely laying down His life. In other words, He, not man, is in control of the timing and circumstances of His death.

Jesus likens His intimate knowledge of His sheep to the relationship He shares with His heavenly Father. Jesus knows His sheep and they know Him, just as the Father knows Jesus and Jesus knows the Father (10:14–15). Jesus also wanted the crowds to know, however, that His sheep were not confined to the people of Israel. This is why Jesus says in verse 16 that He has other sheep that do not belong to this fold—namely, Israel. The other sheep are the Gentiles for whom Christ had also come. But just because Jesus will save Gentiles and Jews does not mean that there are two flocks. Rather, as Jesus says, there will be one flock and one shepherd (10:16). This statement surely anticipates similar ones that the apostle Paul makes, such as in Ephesians 2, where he says that Christ unites both Jew and Gentile into *one* holy temple, and in Romans 11 that the Gentiles were grafted into the *one* olive tree. So, then, Jesus will lead this one flock, and He will lay down His life for His flock to redeem them.

We must remember, though, that Jesus—not the religious leaders—was in control of the time and place of His death. Jesus was not subject to the plans of man, but only to the sovereignty of His Father's will (Acts 2:23). Jesus tells the crowds: "Therefore My Father loves Me, because I lay down My life that I may take it again. No one takes it from Me, but I lay it down of Myself. I have power to lay it down, and I have power to take it again. This command I have received from My Father" (10:17–18). At first glance we might not realize that this is a claim to deity. We have seen the threefold claim of Christ in John 8 where He openly says that He is the great I AM (vv. 12, 28, 58). What about this particular statement in John 10:17–18 tells us it is a claim to deity? It is Jesus's claim that He will lay down His life and take it up again. Not only does Jesus say that He will decide when to lay down His life but, even more amazingly, He also says that He will take it up again. In other words, it is one thing for a person to say that he will take his own life, though even then such things are still subject to the providence of God. However, it is entirely another thing for a person to say that he will come back to life. God alone is the author and giver of life, and once a person is dead, he has no ability to decide what happens to him. In complete contrast, Jesus not only says He will decide when He dies but also will come back to life. This is a veiled statement regarding His resurrection from the dead. Who else but God could make such a claim? We must not forget that Jesus makes this claim wearing Ezekiel's prophecy that Yahweh Himself would shepherd Israel.

We should also not miss the all-important point in this statement—that Jesus is not a victim. Rather, Jesus lays down His life willingly, voluntarily, and because of His great love for His sheep. But He also lays down His life because this is the command of His Father (10:18). In the words of the apostle Paul: "[Christ Jesus], being in the form of God, did not consider it robbery to be equal with God, but made Himself of no reputation, taking the form of a bondservant, and coming in the likeness of men. And being found in appearance as a man, He humbled Himself and became obedient to the point of death, even the death of the cross" (Phil. 2:6–8).

We should not be surprised that after Jesus said these things, the crowd was divided (10:19). Some believed that He was either insane or demon possessed (10:20). Others countered that Christ's words were not those of a demon-possessed man. They asked how a demon-possessed man

could heal a blind man (10:21). At this point, notice who
is missing from the closing of this section: the religious
leaders. Rather than repent of their sin and acknowledge
Jesus to be the Messiah, the true shepherd of the sheep,
they are nowhere to be found. They let the crowd floun-
der on the rocks of their own unbelief and blasphemy.

The Sheep

In many respects there is a world of contrast between
the religious leaders and Jesus—the bad shepherds and
the good shepherd who lays down His life for the sheep.
Although this conflict developed between Jesus and the
religious leaders, it continues in our own day. There are
numerous pastors in churches scattered throughout the
world who look out not for the interests of their flock,
but for their own interests. They promote themselves and
build little fiefdoms—temples to their own egos, a micro-
cosmic universe that revolves around the radiant light of
their own personality. There is no church or denomina-
tion too large or too small to be immune to this type of
bad shepherding.

Good shepherds are those who ultimately point away
from themselves and continually point their sheep to the
one true shepherd. A good shepherd will constantly point
his flock to Jesus, the one who has laid down His life for
His sheep. The sheep will recognize the voice of the one
true shepherd in the reading of and especially the preaching of the Word of God. This is why it is often tempting
for pastors to want to assume the role that only Christ
can fill. People come to them for help, guidance, and

counsel as well as look to them for help in understanding the Scriptures.

However, pastors must constantly aim to die to themselves and point their sheep to Christ in word and in deed. Pray, therefore, for your shepherds, that they would continually point Christ's sheep to the good shepherd who lays His life down for them. But this message is also relevant for husbands, wives, parents, and even children. Parents, do you strive continually to point your little flock to the one true shepherd? Husbands, do you lay down your lives for your little flock (Eph. 5:25–33)? Wives, do you seek to lay down your lives for your little flock, for your husband and children? Do you continually point them to the one true shepherd, Jesus, the one who has laid down His life for His sheep? Do you point your families to Christ, the good shepherd, by praying for them, letting your children see you in prayer, and confessing your sins? Do you lay down your life in sacrificial service for your extended family, friends, and even coworkers? Everyone in the church must seek, by God's grace, to bear the image, characteristics, and sacrificial love of their good shepherd.

Conclusion

As we seek to show others the love that we have received and point them to the good shepherd who lays down His life for the sheep, we should be filled with joy, thanksgiving, and praise. We have not been left to the self-serving plans of man, whether in the world or even in the church. Instead, God Himself, as Moses and Ezekiel prophesied, has come in the person of His Son, Jesus, the good shepherd, not only to lead us out from the dominion of Satan, sin, and death but also to give us life. His death has freed us from our bondage, and, indeed, Jesus not only leads us but is also the door through which we must enter. In this light, we can read the famous Twenty-Third Psalm in a richer way. In the light of Christ's claim, we can gain great comfort from it:

> [Jesus] is my shepherd;
> I shall not want.
> He makes me to lie down in green pastures;
> He leads me beside the still waters.
> He restores my soul;
> He leads me in the paths of righteousness
> For His name's sake.
>
> Yea, though I walk through the valley of the
>   shadow of death,
> I will fear no evil;
> For You are with me;
> Your rod and Your staff, they comfort me.
>
> You prepare a table before me in the presence of
>   my enemies;
> You anoint my head with oil;
> My cup runs over.
> Surely goodness and mercy shall follow me
> All the days of my life;
> And I will dwell in the house of the LORD
> Forever.

Indeed, we can most assuredly say that Jesus is the good shepherd, the one who leads us, blesses us, and brings us to the rest of His peaceful pastures. Pray, therefore, that our good shepherd will continually enable us to point others in both word and deed to Him.

▶ **Questions for Further Study**

1. What was the meaning of the shepherd metaphor in the ancient world?

2. What is unique about Jesus as shepherd? What does He do that other "shepherds" do not do?

3. Who else in the Scriptures criticized Israel's shepherds?

4. How does Christ's conduct as our true shepherd shape our conduct as pastors, leaders, or even parents?

CHAPTER 5

The Resurrection and the Life
John 11:1–44

> *Jesus said to her, "I am the resurrection and the
> life. He who believes in Me, though he may die,
> he shall live. And whoever lives and believes in
> Me shall never die. Do you believe this?"*
> —JOHN 11:25–26

I can remember seeing her picture, and it hit me like a ton of bricks—my friend was dead. She had fought a valiant but failed battle against cancer, and now I was attending her funeral and looking at her coffin. I knew I would never see her again, at least in this life. Blessedly, my friend trusted in Christ for her salvation. Despite the gray cloud of death that hung over her funeral, there were rays of light and hope that broke through in the hymns that we sang and especially in the funeral sermon. The pastor pointed the gathered friends and family to Christ. In the face of death we must cling to one of Christ's greatest "I am" claims—"I am the resurrection and the life" (John 11:25). This claim gave me hope in the face of death. I know that one day I will see my friend again because Christ has conquered death. But in Christ's day, this was something that the people of Israel, even the disciples, did not yet understand. So Christ taught His disciples an important lesson by raising Lazarus from the dead.

For those who attended Sunday school while they were growing up, this account brings to mind felt-board images of a mummy-wrapped Lazarus coming out of his tomb. It is certainly an event that fills children's imaginations with awe and wonder at the power of Christ. However, it should also fill adults' minds with awe and wonder at the power of Christ. It is no accident that this event is the pinnacle of Christ's miraculous signs in John's gospel. The miracles leading up to this one were turning water into wine, healing an official's son, healing an invalid, feeding the five thousand, walking on water, and healing a blind man.

Indeed, the other miracles pale in comparison to raising Lazarus. This miracle builds on what Jesus has demonstrated by the other six miracles—He is God in the flesh, and eternal life comes only through Him. I want us to explore this passage so that we understand the significance of this seventh and final sign and how it relates to Christ's claim, "I am the resurrection and the life." This passage shows us the depths of Christ's love for us as well as the hope that He brings to His people in the face of our fiercest enemy, death. Once again, Jesus dons His Old Testament coat of many colors when he raises Lazarus from the dead—an action that brings to mind Israel's prophesied resurrection in Ezekiel 37. Here Jesus does what only God can do, which confirms His identity as the great I AM—God in the flesh.

The Looming Shadow of Death

John begins chapter 11 by telling us that a man named Lazarus was ill—ill unto death, we find out later in the passage. John explains that Lazarus had two sisters, Mary and Martha, and that Mary would anoint Jesus with ointment and wipe His feet with her hair (John 12:3). Lazarus's sisters sent word to Jesus that their brother was gravely ill, but they knew that if Jesus arrived soon, He could heal him. Jesus, however, did not immediately depart upon receiving word of His sick friend but instead said, "This sickness is not unto death, but for the glory of God, that the Son of God may be glorified through it" (11:4). Jesus was not saying that Lazarus would not die but that rather, in the end, death would not have the last word. Jesus therefore stayed two more days in the place where He was. He was not indifferent to the suffering of His friends. Rather, He purposefully waited—He was ultimately following His Father's timetable, not man's. Moreover, Jesus did not rush to His friend because He did not merely want to resuscitate Lazarus—He wanted to raise him from the dead.

After the two days had passed, Jesus was certain that Lazarus was dead and told His disciples that this was the case. He told them that Lazarus had fallen asleep (11:11), but the disciples thought that Jesus meant that he was merely resting (11:12). Then Jesus told them quite plainly, "Lazarus is dead" (11:14). But notice what follows: "And I am glad for your sakes that I was not there, that you may believe" (11:15). Jesus was happy that He was not present to heal Lazarus. He was not cruel or insensitive; He knew that He was going to raise Lazarus from the dead and demonstrate that He is the resurrection and the life, which would be food for the disciples' faith. He knew that only when it is darkest does the light shine most brightly. Against the backdrop of the oppressive darkness of death, Christ would shine the light of His power on His friend.

Jesus Raises Lazarus

When Jesus finally arrived, Martha met Him and told Him that if He had been there, she knows that Lazarus would not have died. But she still had hope that Jesus could do something: "But even now I know that whatever You ask of God, God will give You" (11:22). This is not to say that Martha knew what Jesus would do. She did not intuitively know that Jesus would raise her brother from the dead. In fact, verse 39 indicates that she did not know what was going to happen, even when Jesus ordered the stone removed from Lazarus's grave. Rather, Martha acknowledged that Jesus had a unique relationship with God and that, even in her sadness, her faith in Him was not shaken.

The exchange between Jesus and Martha continued, and Jesus began to unpack the significance of the miracle He was about to perform, which would be a living illustration to prove that He is the resurrection and the life:

"Your brother will rise again."

Martha said to Him, "I know that he will rise again in the resurrection at the last day."

Jesus said to her, "I am the resurrection and the life. He who believes in Me, though he may die, he shall live. And whoever lives and believes in Me shall never die. Do you believe this?'

> She said to Him, "Yes, Lord, I believe that You
> are the Christ, the Son of God, who is to come
> into the world." (11:23–27)

Martha thought that Jesus was pointing her to the resurrection of the dead on the last day, but instead He was
talking about what would occur in a matter of moments.
She missed Jesus's claim to be both the resurrection and
the life. Only God, the I AM, creates life and holds power
over death. The miracle of raising Lazarus from the dead
would prove Jesus's point that He was God in the flesh
and that if people believed in Him, they would receive
eternal life. It is one thing to claim to be able to give life
to others, but it is entirely another thing actually to do it.

Martha did believe that Jesus is the Messiah and the
Son of God, but she still did not realize what was about to
happen. She returned home to let Mary know that Jesus
had arrived. Mary went out to greet Him, but she too was
grief-stricken and bemoaned Jesus's late arrival. She was
not rebuking Jesus but was simply expressing her grief
and sadness and even her faith in Him that He could have
healed her brother. Jesus's response is important: "He
groaned in the spirit and was troubled" (v. 33). This is
one of the few recorded instances of Jesus being troubled.
With two poignant words, John reports that Christ was
also grieved: "Jesus wept" (v. 35). It is possible to be both
saddened and troubled at the same time, as Jesus was here.
The natural question is, why was Jesus troubled? There
are two likely reasons.

First, Jesus saw the pain that His friends were suffering over the loss of their brother and was expressing

His holy ire at His great enemy, death. Second, many did
not believe—people were grieving as though death would
have the final word. The apostle Paul exhorted the Thes-
salonians not to mourn as the world mourns—the world
mourns without hope (1 Thess. 4:13). People were grieving and had no hope—death was wreaking havoc, and this
troubled Christ. His enemy was plundering and robbing
people of hope. That doubters surrounded Christ is evident from verse 37: They asked, "Could not this Man,
who opened the eyes of the blind, also have kept this man
from dying?" The following verse supports the idea that
Jesus was troubled by their doubt and unbelief, saying
that Jesus was "groaning in Himself" (11:38). Jesus then
instructed the people to remove the stone from Lazarus's
tomb, though Martha showed her lack of faith because she
protested that Lazarus had now been rotting in his grave
for the last four days (11:39).

Jesus reminded her that she would see the glory of
God—that Lazarus would rise from the dead. And so the
people moved the stone, and then Jesus prayed to His
Father: "Father, I thank You that You have heard Me. And
I know that You always hear Me, but because of the people
who are standing by I said this, that they may believe that
You sent Me" (11:41–42). Jesus gave thanks to His Father,
knowing that He would hear Him and raise Lazarus from
the dead. Remember that as God in the flesh, Jesus had
the power to raise Lazarus whenever He wanted. He
could have raised Lazarus from the dead from afar, as He
had healed others. Jesus, nevertheless, submitted to the
will of His Father and eventually even submitted to His
Father's will unto death.

Jesus prayed not only to thank His Father but also to show the people that the Father had truly sent Him, something that had been in dispute as recently as in the previous chapter. And so Jesus "cried with a loud voice, 'Lazarus, come forth!'" (11:43). Lazarus arose from the dead and walked out of the tomb. This powerful miracle was a living parable about Jesus's teaching on the resurrection:

> Most assuredly, I say to you, the hour is coming, and now is, when the dead will hear the voice of the Son of God; and those who hear will live. For as the Father has life in Himself, so He has granted the Son to have life in Himself, and has given Him authority to execute judgment also, because He is the Son of Man. Do not marvel at this; for the hour is coming in which all who are in the graves will hear His voice and come forth— those who have done good, to the resurrection of life, and those who have done evil, to the resurrection of condemnation. (John 5:25–29)

By raising Lazarus from the dead, Jesus showed the people in word and deed that He alone had the power and authority to raise the dead. God the Father gave this power and authority to Christ alone.

Jesus showed Martha and the other doubters that He is the resurrection and the life and that, though man might die, anyone who believes in Jesus lives forever: "I am the resurrection and the life. He who believes in Me, though he may die, he shall live" (John 11:25). Remember that Lazarus would die a second time—he was one of a few individuals to die twice in his life. However, when Jesus raised Lazarus, He was giving the people a foretaste of what would happen on the last day. Through this living parable, Jesus also prophesied His own resurrection from the dead. This is a powerful illustration of what Jesus does for those whom He effectually calls through Spirit-wrought preaching of the Word. Through the preached Word, Christ raises to life those who were once spiritually dead. In Pauline terms, the resurrection of Lazarus illustrates what happens when Christ through the Spirit raises a person according to his inner man (see 2 Cor. 4:16; Eph. 4:20–24). Faithful Israelites who witnessed the resurrection of Lazarus would have likely thought of the resurrection of Abraham's son Isaac (Gen. 22:1–19; cf. Heb. 11:19) and especially Ezekiel's vision of the valley of dry bones (Ezekiel 37). Just as Ezekiel prophesied to the valley of dry bones and raised them from the dead, so Christ spoke to Lazarus and raised him from the dead. Christ did what only God promised to do; hence, He told the gathered crowd, "I am the resurrection and the life."

Are We without Hope?

When your sin and death confront you, how do you respond? We should recognize that we have merited death because of our sin (Rom. 6:23). And make no mistake about it, death is a fierce and relentless foe. There is no candy coating this truth—death is a horrible, horrible thing. The fierceness and suffering that man has inflicted on himself and the world through sin and its consequence drove Christ to a holy anger. We must come to grips with how bad the bad news truly is; there is no way for us to escape death on our own. The only way we can escape the consequences of our sin and rebellion against God is to place our faith in Jesus—in His life, death, resurrection, and ascension. For in so doing, we repent of our own sin and look by faith alone to the One who has fulfilled the law on our behalf, died, paid the penalty of the law for us, has been raised, conquered our fierce foe, and has now ascended on high to reign at the right hand of the Father. It was the hope of Christ's resurrection that enabled the apostle Paul to taunt death:

> "O Death, where is your sting?
> O Hades, where is your victory?"
> The sting of death is sin, and the strength of sin is the law. But thanks be to God, who gives us the victory through our Lord Jesus Christ. (1 Cor. 15:55–57)

This means that in the face of death, we are not without hope. Christ's claim "I am the resurrection and the life" should fill you with great optimism and assurance. In the face of death we will undoubtedly mourn the loss of our friends and family. We will grieve and know that it is an unnatural state of affairs that parents have to bury children and that people are tragically killed in the prime of life. As we look into the mirror and see the effects of old age take its toll on us, we recognize that we inch closer and closer to our own deaths. However, though we might mourn and dearly miss the ones we love, at the same time we must not mourn as the world mourns—the world is without hope.

For the world, death is an irreversible exclamation point: it is an ending, and nothing more. The Christian, the one who is joined to Christ, can look at the graves of his loved ones and know that death is not an ending point but merely a transition. As Paul says, it is the planting of a seed, and while the seed must die, what ensues is far more glorious than the seed ever was:

> So also is the resurrection of the dead. The body is sown in corruption, it is raised in incorruption. It is sown in dishonor, it is raised in glory. It is sown in weakness, it is raised in power. It is sown a natural body, it is raised a spiritual body. There is a natural body, and there is a spiritual body. And so it is written, "The first man Adam became a living being." The last Adam became a life-giving spirit. (1 Cor. 15:42–45)

So the Christian grave is not a place of dishonor and shame; Christ has transformed the grave into a place of hope where we can eagerly await the birth of a resurrected loved one. Every Christian grave becomes a furrow in which the bodies of Christians have been sown and from which shall arise the glorified, transformed, and immortal bodies of God's people on the last day. For in that moment, the dreadful consequences of our sin shall finally be overcome, and we shall be completely purged of every last remnant of rebellion and perfectly reflect the glory of the risen and glorified Christ, who is the resurrection and the life, in our immortal bodies.

Conclusion

In the face of death, look to the resurrected and ascended Christ. In the face of death pray that God the Father would bolster your faith in Jesus, His Son, through God the Holy Spirit. When you mourn, never mourn as the world mourns, but look to Christ and know that your mourning will give way to immeasurable and eternal joy. Sing these truths to your soul! Remember the words of Christ, "I am the resurrection and the life."

▶ **Questions for Further Study**

   1. What is the relationship between Christ's claim "I am the resurrection and the life" and His miracle of raising Lazarus from the dead?

   2. Why did Jesus wait to visit Lazarus? Why did He not immediately rush to His friend?

   3. Why was Jesus troubled by the conduct of the people around Him (see John 6:38)?

CHAPTER 6

The Way, the Truth, and the Life

John 14:1–14

Jesus said to him, "I am the way, the truth, and the life. No one comes to the Father except through Me."
—JOHN 14:6

In their studies, theologians have sometimes tried to describe God by saying what He is not (the way of negation). God is not finite; He is infinite. God is not bound by time; He is atemporal, independent of time. Other theologians have tried to describe God by identifying the best characteristics and qualities in man and ascribing them to God in an elevated way (the way of eminence). Man can love, but God loves in a far greater way. Man is wise, but God is all-wise—omnisapient. Theologians have also asked the question of whether God is transcendent or imminent. This is not to question whether He is one or the other, but rather which attribute is most prominent. That many God-fearing, well-intended theologians have wrestled with these questions does not mean they have started in the correct place. The starting point on a journey is as important as the destination. In this case some of the most brilliant theologians in the history of the church have said that man must first understand God's being.

Francis Turretin, a brilliant Reformed theologian, said that we can never know God as He is in His own being. If we can never know God as He is in His being, then how are we ever to know Him?

Turretin explained that the only way we can know God is through divine revelation, and He has chiefly revealed Himself through Christ and the covenants. In other words, God has successively revealed Himself through the various covenants He has made with His people, but the pinnacle of that revelation is Jesus Christ. This truth may not seem all that profound, but numerous theologians over the ages have missed it, and, even to this day, numerous Christians do not give sufficient weight to this idea. But the idea that Christ chiefly reveals God is not the brilliant insight of Turretin alone but is ultimately the teaching of Christ. We find this teaching scattered throughout John's gospel, and particularly at the beginning of John 14. Let us give our attention, therefore, to what Christ says, that we might know who God is. Indeed, Jesus identifies Himself as the way, the truth, and the life and the only way that we can have access to the Father. As Jesus dons His coat of Old Testament colors, He shows us that He alone reveals the one true God of Israel, the God of the Shema, "Hear, O Israel: The LORD our God, the LORD is one!" (Deut. 6:4). Jesus is God in the flesh and hence is the way, the truth, and the life.

Jesus Reveals the Father

This passage comes on the heels of Peter's famous, well-intentioned, but nonetheless flesh-empowered statement that he would lay down his life for Christ. Jesus responded to Peter's audacious statement with a bold counterclaim of His own—Peter would betray Him three times. People typically follow strong personalities, and Peter was certainly one of the more prominent disciples, along with James and John. If Jesus had told only Peter, one of the Twelve's leaders, that he would betray Christ, then what would have happened to the rest of the disciples? Hence, Jesus comforts His disciples: "Let not your heart be troubled; you believe in God, believe also in Me" (John 14:1). In this passage we find the first clue of Turretin's insightful explanation of how we come to know God. Jesus tells His disciples not to be troubled, but to believe in both God and Him. This is the first indicator that Jesus and the Father are one—that Jesus reveals the Father.

Jesus tells the disciples that He will depart, but it will be to go and prepare a place for them. He will prepare heaven for the reception of His bride. On the heels of this statement we hear "doubting" Thomas, who asks, "Lord, we do not know where You are going, and how can we know the way?" (14:5). Thomas especially (and probably all the disciples) is thinking in spatial or geographical terms, and while it is true that heaven is a place, he was missing Jesus's point. Jesus was not telling the disciples to get up and physically follow Him to heaven. Rather, Jesus's response points Thomas and the disciples to Him as the necessary object of their faith: "I am the way, the truth, and the life. No one comes to the Father except through Me" (14:6). Jesus identifies Himself as the way, which means that He is the road people must travel in order to be saved.

Jesus says that He is the truth. But in what way is He the truth? Jesus is the truth because He narrates God. No one has ever seen God but Jesus, and Jesus alone has made Him known (John 1:18). Jesus does exactly what the Father commands, and only what the Father commands (John 5:19). Jesus is truth incarnate; hence, He reveals God. As John powerfully explains at the beginning of his gospel:

> In the beginning was the Word, and the Word was with God, and the Word was God....
>
> And the Word became flesh and dwelt among us, and we beheld His glory, the glory as of the only begotten of the Father, full of grace and truth. (John 1:1, 14).

These are the ways that Jesus is the truth—the chief revelation of the one true God. But Jesus also said He is the life. How is this so? Jesus is the life because He has life in Himself, has conquered death, and is therefore the resurrection—the source of life for all who look to Him by faith alone (John 5:26; 11:25). Alluding to Old Testament concepts such as creation by saying, "I am...the life," Jesus explains that He is God incarnate, the Creator of heaven and earth. In fact, John tells us this earlier in his gospel: "All things were made through Him, and without Him nothing was made that was made. In Him was life, and the life was the light of men" (John 1:3–4).

So when Thomas tells Jesus he does not know the way to where He is going, Jesus tells him and the rest of the disciples that they do indeed know the way—He is the way. He is the way to the one true God of the Shema

(Deut. 6:4). Jesus is the truth and the life. Jesus is the one way through whom people may be saved and know God the Father: "If you had known Me, you would have known My Father also; and from now on you know Him and have seen Him" (John 14:7). Jesus draws the amazing but nevertheless logical conclusion from all that He has said before—that to see and know Him is to see and know the Father, to see and know the one true God.

Despite Jesus's clarity, Philip, taking over Peter's usual pattern of offering bold but shortsighted speeches, tells Jesus to show them the Father (14:8). Philip and the disciples get in the long line of people, which famously includes Moses, who wanted to see God. Yet he has missed the point that Jesus is making: they are beholding the Father in Jesus! We must remember how troubled Jesus was when this conversation takes place—it is the eve of His crucifixion. Yet He takes the time to explain:

> Have I been with you so long, and yet you have not known Me, Philip? He who has seen Me has seen the Father; so how can you say, "Show us the Father"? Do you not believe that I am in the Father, and the Father in Me? The words that I speak to you I do not speak on My own authority; but the Father who dwells in Me does the works. Believe Me that I am in the Father and the Father in Me, or else believe Me for the sake of the works themselves. (14:9–11)

Jesus reiterates what He has just said. He emphasizes the point: "I reveal the Father." This point is one of the more crucial for understanding who God is.

Notice what else Jesus says. He tells His disciples and, by extension, the church, "Most assuredly, I say to you, he who believes in Me, the works that I do he will do also; and greater works than these he will do, because I go to My Father" (14:12). Jesus tells us that because of His ascension and enthronement, He will enable the church to do greater works than He Himself has done. What Jesus is saying is that the church would see far more people saved and would spread the gospel farther than Christ was able to during His life on earth. But remember that ultimately Christ works through the church.

Jesus tells His disciples and the church that because of their union with Him and His union with the Father, they too would possess the power of the living God through the Holy Spirit: "Whatever you ask in My name, that I will do, that the Father may be glorified in the Son. If you ask anything in My name, I will do it" (14:13–14). The church would share in the power of God through Christ, which is why Jesus says that the church could ask anything in the name of Christ and He would do it. Remember, though, when He says *anything*, it must be defined by what Christ Himself has done. The church would do greater works than Christ, and Christ's works were those that glorified the Father. Hence, whatever the church asks that is consistent with the glorification of the Father, Christ would do in response to the church's prayers.

Seeing God through Christ and His Cross

If we return to the issues that I raised in the chapter introduction and ask what the best way to describe God is, the answer that Jesus gives us is, look at Him. If we want to know about the power of God, we can certainly see it in creation—we can know that God is all-wise from its intricacy and beauty. But the supreme revelation of God's power is manifest in Christ—in His weakness and suffering. If we want to know about the love of God, we do not look to man to find its highest form; rather, we cast our gaze on the cross of Christ, where we see the crucified God-man dying in love for fallen sinners.

If we want to know about the wisdom of God, we do not search the world for sages and philosophers but instead look to Christ, who is Wisdom incarnate. In short, if we want to see and know the Father, we must look to Christ. Lutheran theologian Gerhard Forde describes how we must behold God through the revelation of Jesus, which gives us His cross as one of the chief focal points:

> Theologians of glory are thus always driven to seek transcendent meaning, to try to see into the invisible things of God. They look at the cross and ask, "What is it all about?" They wonder what is "behind" it all. There is a reason for this, of course. If we can *see through* the cross to what is supposed to be behind it, we don't have to *look at* it! It is, finally, a matter of self-defense.[1]

God does not grant access to His invisible essence but instead bids us to cast the eyes of our faith on Christ and His cross. We do not, therefore, have access to God except through Jesus, the way, the truth, and the life, the

---

1. Gerhard Forde, *On Being a Theologian of the Cross* (Grand Rapids: Eerdmans, 1997), 76.

Creator who was crucified by lawless hands. We can never dispense with Jesus or His cross. Indeed, by the Spirit's regenerative power, the cross of Christ corrects our faulty vision—our efforts to seek salvation through other means.

So we must realize that if we want to know who God is, we must travel the road of Christ—for He is the way, the truth, and the life. If man wants to be saved from his sinful condition, the only one to whom he can and must turn is Jesus Christ. There are not multiple ways of salvation, one for each culture, one suited for each individual. No, we all must be conformed to the way of the cross, to the way of Christ. We must all die to ourselves, repent, turn from our sin, and believe on the One whom the Father has sent. We must realize that Jesus does not merely set an example, as one whom we must imitate. Nor is Jesus merely a great teacher who shows us the truth or shows us how we can find eternal life, as if He sets medicine before sick people.

This "I am" text does not allow us to sideline Christ's claim to be the exclusive way to gain access to God the Father. In his famous book *Mere Christianity*, C. S. Lewis explains that when Christ claims to be the only way to the Father, He does not leave us any other choice. We cannot say Jesus was a good moral teacher or something less than the only way—merely one of many ways to God. Lewis's explanation is worth quoting in full:

> I am trying here to prevent anyone saying the really foolish thing that people often say about Him: I'm ready to accept Jesus as a great moral teacher, but I don't accept his claim to be God. That is the one

thing we must not say. A man who was merely a man and said the sort of things Jesus said would not be a great moral teacher. He would either be a lunatic—on the level with the man who says he is a poached egg—or else he would be the Devil of Hell. You must make your choice. Either this man was, and is, the Son of God, or else a madman or something worse. You can shut him up for a fool, you can spit at him and kill him as a demon or you can fall at his feet and call him Lord and God, but let us not come with any patronizing nonsense about his being a great human teacher. He has not left that open to us.[2]

Christ's "I am" claim leaves us only one of three options: He is Lord, a liar, or a lunatic.

Conclusion

Ponder Christ's words. Meditate on the reality that Christ reveals God, that He is the way, the truth, and the life. If we are drawn to acknowledge God before men apart from Christ, then we have given Him no praise. If we are tempted to talk of the love, truth, power, and wisdom of God apart from Christ, we have not talked about God. If we are enticed to talk about God's mercy in the possibility of other ways to be saved, then we have not spoken the truth—we have not spoken of Christ. Christ is *the* way, *the* truth, and *the* life.

---

2. C. S. Lewis, *Mere Christianity* (San Francisco: Harper San Francisco, 2015), 50.

▶ **Questions for Further Study**

1. How does Jesus reveal the Father?

2. Why is Christ's cross so important for our understanding of who God is?

3. What is the difference between the theology of glory and the theology of the cross?

4. What is C. S. Lewis's "trilemma"?

CHAPTER 7

The True Vine
John 15:1–11

"I am the true vine, and My Father is the vinedresser."
—JOHN 15:1

Before I depart on a trip, my wife and I frequently run through a checklist of important things. I remind her where I keep the master list of passwords, inform her to keep an eye out for expected packages, and tell her where I have put all my travel information. Conversely, my wife reminds me of things that I need to do before I leave, such as fill up the car with gas, pay the bills that are due while I am away, or create a packing list so I do not forget anything. On the eve of a departure, you tend to address important matters because you will be unable to take care of them when you are away.

On the eve of His crucifixion, Jesus sat in the upper room with His disciples and told them many important things because they were unprepared for the dramatic and seismic events that were about to occur. Moreover, Christ was also preparing His disciples for His eventual departure after His resurrection. They would undoubtedly look back on this night and recall, reflect, and, under divine inspiration, write about the things that Jesus told them. John covers the events of the Last Supper from

chapters 13 through 17, which is where we find one of the
last of Christ's "I am" statements. Before Jesus plunged
into the depths of His crucifixion suffering, He wanted
His disciples to know that He is the true vine and they
are branches. He wanted them to know about their vital
union to Him and conveyed it to them in terms of this
vine-and-branches metaphor. But the metaphor was not
simply a piece of creative teaching. Jesus did not rely on
a vine metaphor because the disciples lived in an agrar-
ian culture and would be able to understand His teaching.
Rather, Jesus identifies Himself as the *true* vine, which
stands in stark contrast to Israel, God's vine. In order
to appreciate Jesus's teaching, therefore, we will explore
God's vine, Old Testament Israel; Jesus as the true vine;
and, finally, our identity as branches that are connected to
the one true vine.

The Vine

There are many different images that the Old Testament
uses to describe Israel—God's firstborn son, God's wife, a
nation of priests, a dove, and God's flock. Among these is
perhaps a lesser-known image, Israel as a vine. This particular image appears in Psalm 80:

> You have brought a vine out of Egypt;
> You have cast out the nations, and planted it.
> You prepared room for it,
> And caused it to take deep root,
> And it filled the land....
>
> Return, we beseech You, O God of hosts;
> Look down from heaven and see,

And visit this vine
And the vineyard which Your right hand has
     planted,
And the branch that You made strong for Yourself.
     (vv. 8–9, 14–15)

There are many negative images that the Old Testament uses to describe Israel. Israel is God's stiff-necked and rebellious firstborn son, His adulterous wife, a nation of unholy priests, a silly dove, and His straying flock. We can safely assume, therefore, that Israel is not the best of vines.

The prophet Isaiah presents a parable to his fellow countrymen in which he likens Israel to a vine (Isa. 5:1–7). God possessed a vineyard on a fertile hill. He dug it and cleared it of stones and anything that would hamper the growth of what He planted. He built a watchtower, hewed out a wine vat, planted His grapevine, and then eagerly watched and waited for His vineyard to grow. But much to His displeasure, the vine that He planted yielded wild grapes (5:1–2). Wild grapes are sometimes inedible, and those that are edible are typically small and sour, which means they are useless to make wine. In fact, left unchecked, some wild grapevines can become troublesome, uncontrollable weeds.[1] What did God do?

He entered into a lawsuit against His vine and appealed to the people of Israel to resolve the conflict. He called Israel to judge between Him and His vineyard (5:3–4). What did God do with His useless vineyard? He decided

---

1. Carey Ellen Walsh, *The Fruit of the Vine: Viticulture in Ancient Israel* (Winona Lake, Ind.: Eisenbrauns, 2000), 87–94.

to raze it. He would remove its protective hedge and break down its wall, which would allow man and animal alike to trample it down (5:5). Moreover, God would not allow anyone to prune, hoe, or tend it and instead would allow briars and thorns to proliferate in His once carefully manicured vineyard. God would also turn the sky into an iron dome and allow no water to rain down on His vineyard—it would become a haunt, a wasteland (5:6).

If it was not immediately evident from his parable, Isaiah made it abundantly clear to his countrymen who, precisely, was the vine:

> For the vineyard of the LORD of hosts is the
>   house of Israel,
> And the men of Judah are His pleasant plant.
> He looked for justice, but behold, oppression;
> For righteousness, but behold, a cry for help. (5:7)

Israel was the vineyard and the vine planted therein, and instead of yielding the fruit of righteousness and holiness, this vineyard produced the wild grapes of bloodshed, sin, and idolatry. By this parable Isaiah was also prophesying and informing his fellow countrymen that God would carry Israel into exile—He would tear down His vineyard and remove the wicked vine. The prophet Ezekiel prophesies through the same vine metaphor and explains what happens to useless vines: "Son of man, how is the wood of the vine better than any other wood, the vine branch which is among the trees of the forest? Is wood taken from it to make any object? Or can men make a peg from it to hang any vessel on? Instead, it is thrown into the fire for fuel; the fire devours both ends of it, and its middle is burned" (Ezek. 15:2–4). Useless vines, whether those that produce wild grapes or those that are fruitless, are ultimately good for only one thing—fuel for the fire.

The True Vine
In this famous "I am" statement, Christ once again draws from the Old Testament and says, "I am the true vine, and My Father is the vinedresser" (John 15:1). This statement is a locomotive engine that pulls a great deal of Old Testament freight. Loaded on each of the many Old Testament freight cars is the idea that Israel is God's vine. Christ identifies His Father as the vinedresser, which certainly fits Isaiah's parable. The Father planted Israel and tended, watered, and waited for it to produce fruit. It is important that Jesus adds a qualifier, an adjective, to His own identity in the vine discourse. His Father is simply the vinedresser—He has the same role in the Old Testament as He does in the New. But Jesus is the *true* vine. Jesus adds this qualifier to distinguish Himself from Israel. Israel was God's vine that yielded wild grapes—bloodshed, injustice, sin, and idolatry. Jesus, in contradistinction, is the *true* vine—the one who will yield the fruit of love, righteousness, and faithfulness.

Numerous passages of Scripture attest to the fruitfulness of Christ's life. Just a few chapters after the vineyard parable, Isaiah gave his countrymen a message of hope. He said that though they would lay in exile and it would appear as though God had forgotten His covenant promise and that one of David's descendants would rule on Israel's throne (2 Sam. 7:12–16), nevertheless a shoot would come forth from the stump of Jesse, "and a Branch shall grow out of his roots" (Isa. 11:1). From beneath the rubble, thorns, and briars of God's vineyard, a shoot would emerge. The Spirit would rest on this descendant of Jesse, and He would fear the Lord, judge with equity, and wear a belt of righteousness and gird his loins with a belt of faithfulness (Isa. 11:3–5; cf. 32:14–17; 44:2–4). Righteousness is obedience to God's law (Deut. 6:25). Isaiah prophesied that the shoot from the stump of Jesse, then, would be a man who would faithfully obey God's law.

The New Testament clearly identifies Jesus as this righteous and obedient descendant of David. The apostle Paul, for example, states that Jesus descended from David (Rom. 1:3). And Jesus told the gathered crowds when He gave His Sermon on the Mount that He did not come to abolish the Law and the Prophets but to fulfill them (Matt. 5:17). This is why Paul reminds us that Jesus was born of a woman, born under the law, to redeem those who were under the law (Gal. 4:4–5). Jesus was born under the law in order to fulfill it that He might secure the redemption of the elect from every tribe, tongue, and nation. Paul writes: "For if by the one man's offense death reigned through the one, much more those who receive abundance of grace and the gift of righteousness will reign in life through the One, Jesus Christ" (Rom. 5:17). As God's vine, Israel produced wild fruit—bloodshed, injustice, sin, and idolatry. Jesus, the true vine, produced holy fruit—love, righteousness, and faithfulness. Indeed, Jesus told His disciples that, as the true vine, He loved His Father, which means that He obeyed His commandments (John 15:10).

The Branches

Blessedly, though Jesus identifies Himself as the true vine, this does not mean that He has forgotten His people. Jesus told His disciples, "I am the vine, you are the branches. He who abides in Me, and I in him, bears much fruit; for without Me you can do nothing" (John 15:5). Christ, the true vine, transforms His people so that they too produce fruit. By being united to Christ, they produce the fruit of righteousness and faithfulness. We must not miss this vital link—you can be fruitful only by abiding in Christ, by being in union with Him. Christ's words are clear: "Without Me you can do nothing." Sadly, some believe that mere proximity to Christ will be sufficient for their salvation.

Christ explains this point to His disciples: "Every branch in Me that does not bear fruit He takes away; and every branch that bears fruit He prunes, that it may bear more fruit" (15:2). There are doubtless many people who regularly attend church, listen to sermons, and participate in church functions. From all external appearances, they are united to Christ. But Christ is not interested in maintaining appearances. From the very outset, God planted His vineyard and desired to see fruit. The vine Israel failed in this respect, but Christ, the true vine, succeeded. Thus, everyone who is truly united to Christ through the indwelling of the Holy Spirit will produce fruit. In other words, the only way you will produce the fruit of righteousness is if you have the life-giving sap of the Holy Spirit coursing through your life, and the only way you can have this life-giving sap is if you are united to the true vine, Jesus.

The vinedresser will never tolerate fruitlessness. Every branch united to the true vine must produce fruit because this is the purpose for which Christ came to live in obedience to the law, suffer its curse, die, and rise from the dead to ascend to the right hand of the Father: "You are already clean because of the word which I have spoken to you. Abide in Me, and I in you. As the branch cannot bear fruit of itself, unless it abides in the vine, neither can you, unless you abide in Me" (15:3–4). Christ has saved and united you to Himself in order that you would produce fruit. You do not produce fruit so that you might be united to the vine. This is why Jesus echoes Ezekiel's prophecy when He states that the Father cuts off fruitless branches and casts them into the fire (15:6). But the vinedresser has other activities.

Jesus explains that the vinedresser casts fruitless branches into the fire and prunes fruitful ones: "Every branch that bears fruit He prunes, that it may bear more fruit" (15:2). Our heavenly Father providentially ordains different events in our lives that at times are painful and difficult. Gardeners prune plants for a host of different reasons. They cut away dead, diseased, or unproductive branches. They also prune plants to cause them to grow in a specific direction, which enables the plant, for example, to grow straight rather than crooked. In the pruning process, the gardener never aims to kill the plant but rather targets weak and unwanted areas, which ultimately strengthens and makes the plant more fruitful.

Pruning can be a painful process, however, in the life of the believer. We might at first think that God is out to ruin us or make us miserable. God prunes what we thought was vital to our lives—He removes sinful relationships, idols, and habits—not for our destruction but for our edification and His glory. This is why Christ tells His disciples, "By this My Father is glorified, that you bear much fruit; so you will be My disciples" (15:8). God prunes us, therefore, so that we might glorify and enjoy Him forever.

But this entire pruning process is not one marked by sorrow and dreariness. All too often Christians mistakenly believe that love and obedience are antonyms—polar opposites. The world tells us that obedience certainly entails unhappiness and sadness because it means that we have denied ourselves and submitted our will to another. American author Henry David Thoreau (1817–1862) once observed, "Disobedience is the true foundation of liberty. The obedient must be slaves."[2] Thoreau made this statement to encourage people to disobey unjust authority—he did not want them to be the agents of injustice. But I suspect that many people today characterize authority of any kind as unjust. They want freedom from all those who might try to impose their will on them—they equate love with freedom and place it in antithesis to obedience. Yet the true vine places love at the heart of obedience: "As the Father loved Me, I also have loved you; abide in My love. If you keep My commandments, you will abide in My love, just as I have kept My Father's commandments and abide in His love" (15:9–10).

---

2. As quoted in David Hacket Fisher, *Liberty and Freedom: A Visual History of America's Founding Ideas* (Oxford: Oxford University Press, 2005), 261.

Christ's love for His Father was the heart of His obedience to Him. Contrary to the world's ideas, the Bible recognizes the inseparable and dynamic relationship between love and obedience. When asked what the greatest commandment is, Jesus responded with Deuteronomy 6:5, "You shall love the LORD your God with all your heart, with all your soul, and with all your mind" (Matt. 22:37). Obedience to God does not bring oppression but liberation, freedom, and even joy: "These things I have spoken to you, that My joy may remain in you, and that your joy may be full" (15:11). Every branch vitally connected to the true vine, therefore, knows great joy. How do we receive this joy? By being obedient. How can we be obedient? By abiding in Christ. How do we abide in Christ?

We can abide in Christ only if the Father has grafted us into the true vine, and once we are in the vine, we can abide in Christ only by the grace of God. Remember Christ's words: "Abide in Me, and I in you. As the branch cannot bear fruit of itself, unless it abides in the vine, neither can you, unless you abide in Me" (15:4). The way we strengthen our bond to Christ is through His appointed means: Word, sacrament, and prayer. Christ speaks to us through the preaching of the Word and imparts the Spirit-empowered gospel. He speaks to us through the visible Word in the administration of the sacraments. What the Word is to our ears, the sacraments are to our other senses. And we, in turn, speak to Christ through prayer, and the Holy Spirit carries our words to the heavenly Holy of Holies, and Christ answers our prayers. As Christ told His disciples: "If you abide in Me, and My words abide in you, you will ask what you desire, and it shall be done for you" (15:7). Through the means of grace, the vinedresser exposes us to the Sonlight and waters us through the outpouring of the Spirit, which provides us with vital spiritual nutrients so that we can grow and produce the fruit of holiness and righteousness.

Conclusion

If you struggle with besetting sin such as lust, deception, idolatry, or anger, it might be that you are doing everything you can to avoid the vinedresser. You are united to the true vine, but you want only enough life-giving sap to keep you alive so you can continue to engage in your sinful ways. It could be that instead of exposing yourself to the Sonlight and His life-giving word that you have stunted your growth. Draw near to Christ, and He will draw near to you. Pray to Christ that He would help you overcome your unbelief and rest on the finished work of Christ. Pray that He would send His life-giving sap into your life that you would overcome your besetting sins. Pray and ask the vinedresser to forgive you for kicking against the goads of His providence. Ask for courage that you would not fear His pruning. For when He prunes you, He aims only to remove what is dead, sinful, and crooked so that you would be strengthened, made holy, and grow straight. Abide in Christ, and He will abide in you. Apart from Christ you can do nothing. Christ has loved you and enabled you to love Him and keep His commandments. United to the one true vine, be filled with love and joy and celebrate your privileged place as one united to the true and faithful vine, Jesus Christ.

▶ **Questions for Further Study**

1. Who was the first to use the imagery of a vine for God's people, and where in the Scriptures was this imagery used?

2. Why does Jesus call Himself the *true* vine?

3. How can we, the branches, produce fruit in our lives?

Conclusion:
God in the Flesh

How might you react if you encountered God in the flesh? How would you respond if you looked into the very eyes of God? Most of us can only wonder about such things, but in the last of Jesus's "I am" sayings, we see how one group of people reacted. Jesus was in the garden of Gethsemane praying to His heavenly Father. He was well aware that one of His close, trusted disciples would soon betray him (John 13:26). When Judas finally arrived with a detachment of troops, representatives from the chief priests and Pharisees, Jesus went toward them and asked, "Whom are you seeking?" (John 18:4). The crowd responded that they were seeking Jesus of Nazareth (v. 5). Then Jesus uttered the words, "I am" (v. 5). Once again Jesus donned His Old Testament coat of many colors and invoked the divine name once uttered by Yahweh from the burning bush (Ex. 3:14). His statement here also echoes Isaiah 47:8: "I am, and there is no one else besides me."

John tells us that the crowd was ready for a fight, as they came with "lanterns, torches, and weapons" (John 18:3). The Pharisees probably told the soldiers and the crowd that Jesus's disciples would put up a fight and resist them with force, and Peter was prepared to do this, as

he struck the high priest's servant and cut off his ear—
likely aiming for his head (18:10). Nevertheless, even
though they were armed, when Jesus uttered the words,
"I am" (*ego eimi*), the crowd "drew back and fell to the
ground" (18:6).

Why did the soldiers fall at the mere utterance of these
two words? Probably, they were aware of all the miracles
that Jesus had performed, such as raising Lazarus from
the dead—they were aware that Jesus was more powerful than any mere man. It is likely that this knowledge,
combined with the utterance of the divine name, caused
the soldiers and crowd to react with fear and reverence
because they were standing in the presence of God in the
flesh. The crowd's reaction is also ironic: Jesus, a lone,
unarmed man faced an armed mob, yet as these words
come from His mouth, they fall back in fear. Once they
were able to gather their senses and renew their sinful
resolve, they sadly did not act on their initial impulse to
fear God in the flesh. Jesus asked them again, "Whom are
you seeking?" and the crowd again responded, "Jesus of
Nazareth" (18:7). Jesus again told them, "I have told you
that I am," and asked that they let His disciples go (v. 8).
The crowd eventually looked God in the eyes and arrested
Him to hold a trial in a kangaroo court and crucify the
Lord of glory. Rather than walk in the light, the crowd
would rather retreat to the darkness of their wickedness
and ignore the reality of who Jesus is.

If you were uncertain about Christ's identity before
you began this study, hopefully John has left you without
doubt. Often we read John's gospel and do not realize the
significance of all the things that Jesus told His disciples.

We do not recognize much of what He says because we do not realize that He is wearing His Old Testament coat of many themes, passages, and colors. Each of the "I am" sayings is rich with allusions and echoes to the Old Testament.

John	Claim	Old Testament Connection
6:20	Do not be afraid. I AM.	Only Yahweh walks on the water, but Jesus walks on the water and tells the disciples not to fear because He is I AM.
6:35, 48	I am the bread of life.	Jesus draws the crowd's attention to the exodus, when God fed Israel with manna from heaven. Jesus tells the crowds that He too is from heaven and that God intends to feed them with His Son, the bread of life.
8:12	I am the light of the world.	During the Feast of Tabernacles, Jesus invokes the exodus, particularly the theme of the pillar of fire guiding Israel by night. Israel identified the pillar with Yahweh, but now Jesus tells the crowds that He is the light of the world, not just of Israel.
8:24	If you do not believe that I AM, you will die in your sins.	This is the first of three instances in which Jesus claims the divine name for Himself at the Feast of Tabernacles.

John	Claim	Old Testament Connection
8:28–29	When you lift up the Son of Man, then you will know that I AM.	This is the second of three instances where He claims the divine name.
8:58	Before Abraham was, I AM.	This is the third of three instances where Jesus claims the divine name for Himself, and the crowd finally understands this and wants to kill Him for it.
10:9	I am the door.	Jesus identifies Himself as the only way to enter the sheepfold of God. God's people as His sheep is a common Old Testament image.
10:11	I am the good shepherd.	Jesus identifies Himself as the good shepherd, which undoubtedly draws the crowd's mind to Psalm 23. They would have connected this with Yahweh, but now Christ is claiming to be the one and only shepherd.
11:25	I am the resurrection and the life.	Only God can give life. To prove He is God and was sent by His Father, Jesus raises Lazarus from the dead, which echoes passages such as Ezekiel 37 and the valley of dry bones.
14:6	I am the way, the truth, and the life.	Jesus claims that He alone grants access to the Father, the God of Israel's Shema (Deut. 6:4). He also echoes Genesis 1 when He claims to be the life—a title worthy of the Creator.

John	Claim	Old Testament Connection
15:1	I am the true vine.	Invoking Old Testament prophetic imagery of Israel as God's vine, Jesus identifies Himself as the true vine. Only by being united to the true vine can we find salvation and fruitful existence.
18:5–6, 8	I AM	Jesus invokes the divine name when the mob comes to arrest Him, echoing Exodus 3:14 and Isaiah 47:8–9.

Jesus was abundantly clear about His identity; He did not hide the fact that He was God in the flesh. John explained in the opening verses of his gospel that "in the beginning was the Word, and the Word was with God, and the Word was God" (1:1). But then he explained in the rest of the gospel that Jesus made specific claims—He invoked the divine name and claimed to be the great I AM in word and deed. Moreover, He also abundantly proved that He alone is the only Savior of both Jew and Gentile.

Sadly, the typical reactions to Christ's claims were anger, doubt, blasphemy, and outright hatred. The crowd's rejection culminated in their fateful response to Pilate's question about whether he should crucify their King. The crowd shouted angrily, "We have no king but Caesar!" (John 19:15). The crowds spoke more than they knew. Pilate, however, saw that a sign was posted over Christ's cross in Hebrew, Greek, and Latin: "JESUS OF NAZA-RETH, THE KING OF THE JEWS" (John 19:19). The religious leaders objected, but Pilate was unmoved by their request (John 19:21–22). John's point is clear—Jesus is the great I AM. Jesus has made this explicit claim six times in John's gospel (6:20; 8:24, 28, 58; 18:5, 8), and He has abundantly demonstrated His identity by clothing Himself in His Old Testament coat of many colors.

We cannot sit idly by and think that Jesus was a great moral teacher or that the church misunderstood His claims and mistakenly elevated Him to a deity. If we listen to Christ's claims and the accounts of His actions with our ears tuned to the frequencies of the Old Testament, we will receive the message loud and clear. Like C. S. Lewis observed, we must, therefore, reject Christ's claims and believe Him to be a liar. Only a demon would claim to be God when he was not. We could also believe that He was a lunatic. Who else but a madman would claim to be God when he was not? Or, we must fall on our faces and worship Him as Lord. John's intent is clear—we must fall on our faces and worship the one true living God who was made flesh and dwelled among men that He might seek and save the lost.

I will close with a parting thought from John's gospel, something that has deep roots in the Old Testament. When Jesus was speaking to the crowds during the Passover, the religious leaders had reached their tipping point. They were now planning to assassinate Him and murder Lazarus; many had believed because of the great miracle of raising him from the dead (John 12:9–11). Jesus rode on a young donkey and triumphantly entered Jerusalem as had been prophesied in the Old Testament (12:14–15). The Pharisees were incensed, to say the least (12:19), so they began interrogating Jesus as they had done on numerous occasions before (12:34). Jesus patiently answered their questions, but to no avail—they were hardened in their hatred and disbelief. John then comments: "But although He had done so many signs before them, they did not believe in Him, that the word of Isaiah the prophet might be fulfilled" (12:37–38). John then quotes the damning indictment against Israel in Isaiah's day:

> Lord, who has believed our report?
> And to whom has the arm of the LORD been
>   revealed?…
>
> He has blinded their eyes and hardened their
>   hearts,
> Lest they should see with their eyes,
> Lest they should understand with their hearts
>   and turn,
> So that I should heal them. (12:38–40)

John offers some of the most amazing words in his gospel: "These things Isaiah said when he saw His glory and spoke of Him" (12:41). Whose glory did Isaiah see? And whose glory did Isaiah speak of? Within the broader context of this passage there is only one subject—Jesus. John clearly tells us, therefore, that Isaiah made these prophetic declarations about Israel when he saw *Christ* in the temple! Isaiah's famous vision in chapter 6 of his book is not a theophany, an appearance of God in the Old Testament, but rather a christophany—an appearance of the preincarnate Christ. On what Isaiah thought was an ordinary day, Christ shattered his expectations by unfurling His thrice-holy preincarnate glory:

> In the year that King Uzziah died, I saw the Lord
> sitting on a throne, high and lifted up, and the train
> of His robe filled the temple. Above it stood sera-
> phim; each one had six wings: with two he covered
> his face, with two he covered his feet, and with two
> he flew. And one cried to another and said:
>
> > "Holy, holy, holy is the LORD of hosts;
> > The whole earth is full of His glory!"
>
> And the posts of the door were shaken by the
> voice of him who cried out, and the house was
> filled with smoke. (Isa. 6:1–4)

The seraphim attended the Son of God, and the sight of
Christ's unfettered glory drove Isaiah to call a curse upon
his own head, for he knew that he was sinful. He was in
desperate need of Christ's grace so that he might stand
in His presence unharmed. One of the seraphim tended
to Isaiah and cleansed him from his sin by touching his
lips with a coal from the altar. Isaiah would then go forth,
commissioned by the preincarnate Christ, to herald his
prophetic message of judgment.

This same glorious Christ, who is served by the angels
of heaven who antiphonally herald His holiness and glory,
is the same God who condescended to dwell among men:
"And the Word became flesh and dwelt among us, and
we beheld His glory, the glory as of the only begotten of
the Father, full of grace and truth" (John 1:14). Throughout His ministry Jesus walked the dusty roads of Israel,
ate with sinners, and patiently endured the persecution,
hatred, and revilement of the unbelieving crowds, of His
own countrymen. In the various events of Jesus's ministry,

He told and showed the crowds who He truly was—He donned His Old Testament coat of many colors and told them quite plainly, "I am the great I AM." The nadir of His humiliation and suffering, however, came during His crucifixion when He hung naked on the cross so that He might bear the sins of the world (John 1:29; 19:23–24). The thrice-holy God, bedecked in royal glory and splendor, whose holiness is so great that the seraphim would not look on Him and covered their eyes with their wings, was now hanging on the cross in ignominy. Indeed, "greater love has no one than this," that Christ should lay down His life for His friends, and that is what you are if you believe in Jesus (John 15:13).

The King of kings and Lord of lords lived, suffered, and died so that you might receive the forgiveness of sins and have eternal life. Will you trust Christ, the great I AM; He who walks on water and treads on the waves; the One who was, is, and is to come? Will you eat the manna from heaven and never hunger again? Will you step into the light of Christ, or continue to walk in darkness? Will you search for other entry points or recognize that Christ is the door and the way, the truth, and the life? Trust in Jesus, the good shepherd who has laid down His life for His sheep. Seek the true vine so that He might produce the fruit of righteousness and holiness in your life. Believe in Jesus so that on the last day, when the last trump sounds, Jesus will call out your name and you will rise from the dead. Jesus is the bread of life, the light of the world, the door, the good shepherd, the resurrection and the life, the way and the truth, and the true vine—in a word, Jesus is the great I AM.